Golden City Tastes & Traditions

Golden, Colorado

Howdy Folks!
WELCOME TO GOLDEN
WHERE THE WEST REMAINS

COOKING
INFORMATION HERE
GOLDEN CHAMBER
OF COMMERCE

Golden Cultural Alliance

Vasquez Forks Waffles Pg. 56
Astor House Museum

Strawberry Sparkle Punch Pg. 36
Clear Creek History Park

Southwest Cheesecake Pg. 199
Foothills Art Center

South Table Strata Pg. 51
Miners Alley Playhouse

Cornish Game Hens Pg. 118
Golden Oldy Cyclery

Corn and Bulgur Salad Pg. 140

Oriental Chicken Salad Pg. 98
Golden Oldy Cyclery

Baked Nut Stuffed Mushrooms Pg. 7
Golden Oldy Cyclery

Chili Dumpling Stew Pg.67
Clear Creek History Park

Roast Beef And Dumplings Pg.106
Astor House Museum

Kraut Relish Pg. 167
Sweet and Sour Mustard Pg.167
Apple Butter Pg.166

Cranberry Relish Pg. 166
Clear Creek History Park

Cranberry Relish Pg.166
Clear Creek History Park

Pear, Walnut and Blue Cheese Salad Pg.92
Shrimp Ceviche Pg.8

Marinated Shrimp and Avocado Pg.95
Foothills Art Center

Zuccanoes Pg. 150
Clear Creek White Water Park

Black Bean Soup Pg.211
Corn and Honey Salad Pg. 94
Clear Creek History Park

Introduction

In the human experience, nothing spells comfort quite as universally as do the kitchen and the hearth. When the Golden Cultural Alliance realized that visitors and residents wanted a "piece" of Golden to be able to take home with them, it seemed natural to provide something that represented the diverse range of activities, the unique flavor of the historic West and the home town friendliness that has traditionally been associated with this very special place.

This book is first and foremost a bounty of home grown culinary delights that will help make the kitchen that warm and comfortable island in your home. At the same time, enjoy the many snippets of history and lore that will provide a smile and some wisdom about Golden and Colorado — where the West truly does live. Finally, the Alliance has attempted to design this treasure as a fine gift or thank you to someone who deserves a special treat.

The more than 250 recipes in this book have been tested for quality. From an initial selection of over 350 offerings, these are the compositions that are of a good quality, easy to prepare if instructions are followed as printed and will yield the flavor or taste indicated. In the west we believe a person is as good as their word, and this volume provides solid value.

We sincerely hope this cookbook becomes an important part of your home and family -

Tastes and Traditions

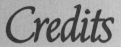

Credits

This cookbook is the team effort of more than 150 people whose community spirit and love of Golden fill the following pages with the "Tastes & Traditions" of OUR Town. The Cookbook Committee wishes to express its sincere appreciation and thanks to all of the following individuals who submitted and/or tested recipes. The following list also identifies the organizations that make up the Golden Cultural Alliance, with special notations thanking other individuals for their technical support.

Astor House Museum
Buffalo Bill Museum and Grave
Chief Hosa Lodge
Clear Creek History Park
Colorado Mountain Club
Colorado Railroad Museum
Daughters of the American Revolution -
      Mt. Lookout Chapter
Foothills Art Center
Friends of Dinosaur Ridge
Golden Chamber Choir
Golden Chamber of Commerce
Golden Landmarks Association
Golden Oldy Cyclery
Golden Pioneer Museum
Golden Public Library
Golden Resource for Education, Arts, &
      Theater, Inc. (GREAT)
Golden Urban Renewal Authority (GURA)
Golden Visitors Center
Jefferson Symphony Orchestra

Lookout Mountain Nature Center
Miners Alley Playhouse
Rocky Mountain Quilt Museum
Mesa Music Fest
Table Mountains Conservation Fund
Michelle Zupan- Cookbook Coordinator
Sarah West - Graphics Designer
Dave Shrum of Colorado Camara - Photographer
Chef Joachim Shaaf, Chris Brinkman,
Krystal Roberts - Food Preparation &
Presentation

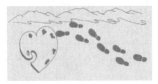

www.goldenculturalalliance.org
www.goldencookbook.org

This cookbook was made possible by major funding from the **Golden Civic Foundation** and additional financial support from the Golden Urban Renewal Authority. Thank you for making Golden City: Tastes & Traditions a reality.

2

Credits

udy Babb
Barber
arol Baroch
arbara Barr
arolyn Bartels
anda Beck
erri Becker
lie Beckwith
ark Beckwith
ick Bernstein
nda Bick
ani Bickart
hirley Bjarnason
arol Born
z Bowers
osalyn Bowers
arol Ann Bowles
izabeth Boxler
ick Boxler
y Brandt
hris Brown
inny Burr
yne Byl
huck Carter
an Cava
argaret Chapman
ene Child
nny Christiansen
aria Cochran
m Conder
ey Corkern
orothy Crawford
erri Crawford
he Crawford Family
ndy Curran
elia Curtis
nda Dean
ony Dean
ti Deland
dy Denison

Rebecca S. Doherty
Bonnie Driste
Kerstin Einwiller
Judy Ellis
Marcie Emily
Helen Erickson
Tracy Evanko
Janet Finley
Dottie Flanagan
Beth Fletcher
Margie Foster
Opal Frey
Steve Friesen
Rick Gardner
Nancy Gelbhaus
Elaine Gendron
Phylis Goss
Katharine Grosenick Topper
Mary Hager
Muriel Handwork
Barb Hanni
Louise Hardesty
Marijane Harlan
Lynda Harris
Jerry Hodgden
Linda Holst
Shelley Howe
Al Huffman
Kathy Husband
Jan Jacobs
Carol Jansons
Annie Jensen
Betty Johnson
Katherine Johnson
Ann Johnston
Annette Kaalund-Jorgensen
Gabrielle Kelly
Patricia Krehbiel
Jean Kuss
Cherryl Lagae

Helen Leith
Rosalyn Lemon
Kim Lennox
Judy Madison
Kimery Marchese
Betsy Martinson
Scotti McCarthy
Mary McGill
Doris McGowan
Myrtle McGrath
Mary McHenry
Norma Medina
Cathy Meis
Sara Michal
Lee Michels
Connie Mondy
Pat Moore
Connie Moudy
Patty Mozena
Barb Mutnan
Kathy O'Connor
Elinor Packard
Joyce Palmer
Don Parker
Mary Parker
Schardelle Paul
Jill Polito
Laura Ragan
Mary Ramstetter
Pat Raub
John Remenar
Nanci Rinehart
Tamara Roghaar
Carma Romano-LaMorte
Barb Rood
Heidi Row
Rourk Ruffing
De Russell
June Ryker
Shirley Sanden

Pary Schluchtner
Pat Schuster
Karen Setzer
Bill Smith
John Spear
Cyndi Spice
John Spice
Alyson Stanfield
Jean Stefanich
Steve Stevens
Sandra Stover
Ginny Sugg
Dorothy Swanson
Beatrice Szadokierski
Donna Taulby
Monika Taylor
Margaret Taylor Aropman
Mary Joyce Thompson
Diane Tiberi
Lori Tigner
Elizabeth Tisinger
Shelly Truitt
Pat Turner
Rhonda VanDriel
Robert Vogel
Vicki Wagner
Robin Walsh
Carol Watson
Sharon Wheatley
Kathy Williams
Marilyn Williams
Joan Wilson
Brenda Witters
Sue Young
Pat Zialkowski
Barb Zimmer

Contents

A Great Start

The Guy Hill School was built between 1874 and 1876 in Golden Gate Canyon. Enrollment varied, but in 1951 it had about 27 pupils from all 12 grades. The school was closed in 1951. It remained vacant until 1976 when the students at Mitchell Elementary in Golden petitioned to have it moved down to their school grounds. The school stood at Mitchell until about 1994 when that school was closed. Guy Hill was moved one last time to serve as the keystone to the Clear Creek History Park in downtown Golden. The Park then added buildings from the Pearce Ranch, such as a homestead cabin and mining cabin, as well as a chicken coop, hay barn, and spring house.

(Photo: Guy Hill School, c.1870; courtesy of the Golden Pioneer Museum)

Washington Avenue Wings

5 lbs. chicken wings
1 tbsp. butter
2 tbsp. honey
1 tsp. maple syrup
10 oz. Frank's Red Hot Sauce*
1 tsp. parsley
1 tsp. chives
1 tsp. red pepper flakes
½ tsp. thyme
½ tsp. poultry seasoning
½ tsp. sage
¼ tsp. garlic powder
dash salt
dash pepper
dash Worcestershire sauce

Prep Time: 10 minutes
Cooking Time: 30 minutes
Serves: 5

Preheat oven to 350°. For each chicken wing, cut off wing end and discard, then cut each wing at joint, so you have two "drummettes." Dry thoroughly. Heat 3 inches of oil in a deep fryer to 400°. Fry each drummette until golden brown. Remove from fryer and drain on paper towel.

In a large bowl, microwave the butter, honey, and syrup until melted. Add remaining spices and herbs. Dip each drummette thoroughly in the sauce mix. Place into greased 14" x 9" baking pan. Bake for 10 minutes.

Serve with blue cheese dressing to cool the fire.

* For a milder appetizer, reduce the amount of Frank's Red Hot Sauce by half.

Baked Nut Stuffed Mushrooms

24 medium-sized mushrooms

2 tbsp. butter or margarine

1 tsp. instant minced onion

½ cup dry bread crumbs (prepared Italian is fine)

¼ cup sliced almonds or Brazil nuts

4-6 strips crisply cooked bacon, crumbled

¼ tsp. salt

6 tbsp. chicken broth or consommé

Rinse, pat dry and remove mushroom stems. Chop stems and lightly sauté in butter 2 minutes. Add onion and sauté 2 minutes longer. Combine with bread crumbs, nuts, bacon and salt. Mix well.

Add chicken broth and stuff mixture into reserved mushroom caps. Place in buttered shallow baking dish and bake at 350°F for 8-10 minutes until heated through. Serve hot as an appetizer or as a side vegetable. Recipe saves at this point for 1 day if kept tightly covered and refrigerated.

Cheese Delights

These spicy snacks go great with beer. Try them for your next party.

½ lb. sharp cheese

1 ½ sticks margarine

1 tbsp. evaporated milk

few drops Tabasco sauce

2 cups flour

1 tsp. sugar

½ tsp. salt

1 tsp. chili powder

½ tsp. ground red pepper

about 40 pecan halves

Preheat oven to 250°. Grate cheese and set aside to soften at room temperature. Cream margarine, then add cheese and mix well. Stir in milk and Tabasco sauce. Sift flour with sugar and spices. Add flour mixture to cheese mixture, mix well. Drop by tablespoon onto lightly greased cookie sheet about ¼ inch apart. Place a pecan half in the center of each. Bake about 40 minutes, or until lightly brown. Yields about 40.

Golden Chamber of Commerce and Visitors Center

1010 Washington Avenue
Golden, Colorado 80401
303-279-3113
Fax 303-279-0332
www.goldencochamber.org

The Golden Chamber of Commerce has been promoting the prosperity and welfare of the greater Golden area since 1920. Over 525 members are committed to a healthy economy involved in competitive free enterprise and the coordination of profession, business and industry.

Shrimp Ceviche

1 pound raw shrimp, peeled and deveined
¾ cup fresh lime juice
4 Anaheim chilies or 6 jalapenos, roasted, peeled and chopped*
2 green onions, diced
½ red onion, diced
3 ripe Roma tomatoes, peeled, seeded, and diced
½ tsp. kosher salt
½ tsp. Mexican oregano (epazote)
2 tbsp. olive oil
1 tbsp. fresh cilantro, chopped

In a glass bowl (do not use metal), cover shrimp with lime juice. Cover and refrigerate 2 hours, stirring one or two times.

Add remaining ingredients; marinate one hour or more, stirring occasionally.

Serve chilled with crackers or tortilla chips.

Serves 6

* To roast your own chilies: Preheat oven to Broil. Place washed and dried chilies on a non-reactive baking sheet. Broil for several minutes until skins begin to blister and split, remove from oven, turn chilies to expose opposite side to broiler, return to oven until skins blister and split. Remove from oven, place into plastic zipper-close bag. Place bag onto surface that will not blister from heat. Cover bag with towels. Wait 20 minutes. Remove chilies from bag. Skins should slip off.

Barbecued Meatballs

This recipe makes a lot! They freeze well. Use ground turkey for a healthier version.

Meatballs:

3 pounds ground beef or turkey
        OR a combination of them
2 cups oatmeal
2 eggs
½ cup chopped onion
2 tsp. salt
¼ tsp. pepper

Sauce:

2 cups catsup
2 cups brown sugar
½ cup chopped onion
2 tbsp. liquid smoke
½ tsp. garlic powder
2 tsp. chili powder
½ tsp. garlic powder

Mix all meatball ingredients together and shape into 1" balls. Place in flat pan in a single layer only. Mix all sauce ingredients together and pour over meatballs. Bake at 350° for 1 hour. Makes 55 large or 110 appetizer meatballs.

Golden Chamber of Commerce and Visitors Center

Continued

The Golden Chamber of Commerce is a non-profit Colorado corporation guided by a voluntary board of directors, with elected officers and coordinated by a paid staff. Financed by members' investments and fund-raisers, the Chamber serves as an information and communication resource center for the greater Golden area. Representing the business community with one independent voice is another responsibility of the Chamber. As a liaison between businesses, and the community, the Chamber works to improve the marketplace, transportation systems and to promote new business and employment.

Beer Cheese

If you don't have a food grinder or processor, just grate the cheese and mix in other ingredients. To make beer stale, pour into a saucepan and heat at medium heat just until warm.

2 lbs. sharp cheese
2 garlic cloves, minced
½ medium onion, minced
1 tsp. Worcestershire sauce
¼ tsp. cayenne pepper
¼ tsp. Tabasco sauce
salt to taste
one bottle of stale beer (approximate)

Run cheese, garlic and onions through food grinder or processor. Add spices and mix well. Slowly add beer a little at a time, beating the mixture until blended and smooth, until the desired consistency is reached. Serve on crackers or as a dip for fresh veggies or chips.

This is a GREAT recipe that's fun to play with. To find the taste that's just right for you, try different kinds of cheese, more garlic or hot sauce, or different kinds of beer.

Breadloaf Barbecue

Great for a potluck as no dishes or serving spoons are required.

1 loaf French bread, long or round loaf, not sliced
1 ½ lbs. lean ground beef
½ cup bread crumbs (or use center of the loaf of bread for the bread crumbs)
1 bottle chili sauce
1 tsp. Worcestershire sauce
1 tsp. vinegar
1 tbsp. chili powder
1 tbsp. horseradish
¼ cup onion, chopped
1 clove garlic, crushed
1 tsp. salt (optional)
pepper to taste

Cut top out of bread to make a lid. Scoop out center of loaf.

Brown beef stirring so mixture is crumbly. Drain excess fat from time to time. When the meat is nearly done, add remaining ingredients and mix well to combine. Stuff into bread loaf and put lid on top. Wrap loaf in foil. Bake 15 minutes at 425° until heated through. Serves 4 - 8.

Chicken Satay

The Colorado School of Mines brings students from all over the world to Golden. This dish comes to Golden from India.

12 - 18 chicken wings
1 tbsp. soy sauce
1 tsp. sugar
1 tsp. lemon juice

2 tbsp. curry powder
Satay Sauce (recipe follows)
vegetable oil

Cut each chicken wing into 3 pieces; discard tips. Place pieces into mixing bowl and cover with soy sauce, lemon juice, sugar, and curry powder. Marinate at least 30 minutes or up to 2 hours. Prepare the Satay Sauce and set aside. Heat oil in a deep fryer to 360°. Place a few wings at a time into the hot oil and fry until brown and crisp. Drain on paper towels. Serve hot or cold with Satay Sauce.

Satay Sauce:
1 large red bell pepper
1 tbsp. vegetable oil
3 tbsp. shallots, sliced thin

2 tbsp. curry powder
1 cup cream of coconut
½ cup chunky peanut butter
1 tsp. sugar

Preheat broiler to high or heat a gas or charcoal grill. Roast the pepper, turning frequently, until skin blisters and chars. Place into paper bag and let stand until cool enough to handle. Peel, core, seed and chop. Heat the oil in a small skillet and saute shallots briefly; add curry powder, cook briefly, then add pepper. Remove to a bowl. In the skillet, bring cream of coconut to simmer; add pepper cubes and shallots. Add peanut butter and sugar. Simmer about 5 minutes, stirring occasionally. Pour the mixture into blender or food processor and blend thoroughly. Return mixture to skillet and bring to simmer. Thin with water or chicken stock if desired.

Clams Casino

Golden was settled in 1859 by men and women from the Eastern Seaboard states. This recipe is a favorite first course for many of today's Easterners in Golden.

3 dozen freshly opened clams
rock salt
3 slices bacon
½ cup scallions, minced
¼ cup green pepper, minced
¼ cup celery minced
1 tsp. lemon juice
1 tsp. Worcestershire sauce
2 drops Tabasco sauce

Preheat oven to 400°. Place 2 drained clams onto one shell; continue with remaining clams. Arrange filled shells on a layer of rock salt in large baking pans. Cook the bacon until crisp; remove from pan and crumble; reserve fat. To the fat in the skillet add scallions, green pepper, and celery. Cook until almost tender. Add lemon juice, Worcestershire sauce, and Tabasco. Spoon mixture into shells on top of clams; then top with bacon. Bake 10 minutes.

Shrimp Remoulade

This is a traditional Creole red remoulade sauce. It is generally served with chilled shrimp or crabmeat, but can be used as a topping for a warm shrimp and pasta dish.

¼ cup lemon juice
¾ cup olive oil
½ cup onion, diced
¼ cup celery, chopped
2 cloves garlic, diced
1 tbsp. horseradish
5 tbsp. spicy brown mustard
3 tbsp. ketchup
2 tbsp. parsley
1 tbsp. cilantro
1 tsp. salt
¼ tsp. cayenne
1/8 tsp. black pepper
1 pound boiled medium shrimp, peeled, deveined, and chilled
romaine or leaf lettuce leaves

Place all ingredients except shrimp and lettuce leaves into a food processor or blender and blend well for 30 seconds. To serve: place a few lettuce leaves on a plate. Then top with 5 or 6 shrimp and a dollop of r'emoulade sauce. Store leftover sauce in the refrigerator.

Hummus

2 cups cooked or canned garbanzo beans, drained
2/3 cup tahini (sesame paste)
¾ cup lemon juice
2 garlic cloves, peeled
salt and pepper to taste
¼ cup scallions, finely diced
paprika

Place garbanzo beans, tahini, lemon juice, garlic, salt and pepper into a food processor and process until smooth. Stir in scallions. Serve in a small bowl or plate topped with a sprinkle of paprika. Serve with pita bread or pita chips.

Mushroom Pate

12 oz. mushrooms
1 tbsp. minced shallots
6 oz. cream cheese
2 tbsp. mayonnaise
1 tbsp. chicken bouillon granules
2 tbsp. fresh parsley, chopped

Slice the mushrooms and sauté in a little butter. Add all of the ingredients to a food processor and blend. Refrigerate overnight. Serve with crackers.

Shrimp Dijon

2 lbs. of pre-cooked shrimp without tails
1/2 cup red wine vinegar
1/4 cup salad oil
1 tsp. salt
1 tsp. dill weed
1 tbsp. yellow mustard
1 tbsp. horseradish
1 large sweet onion, cut in large pieces
6-12 pickled jalapeno pepper pieces with juice

Mix all ingredients and marinate in the refrigerator for 24 hours. Serve with crackers. For added spice, add more jalapeno juice.

Crabmeat Canapés

1 small jar Kraft Olde English Cheddar Cheese Spread
1 stick margarine, softened
1 small can crabmeat
½ tsp. garlic powder
½ tsp. seasoning salt
1 package English Muffins

Let cheese and margarine soften. Drain crabmeat. Mix together all ingredients, stirring until at a spreading consistency. Spread on split English Muffins. Place on cookie sheet and bake in a preheated 350° oven until hot and cheese is melted. Cut each round into 4 small pieces. Serve hot.

Mt. Zion Zucchini Appetizer

4 eggs, beaten

1 cup Bisquick

½ cup grated parmesan cheese

½ cup finely chopped onion

½ cup vegetable oil

½ - 1 tsp. dried parsley, or more fresh parsley

½ tsp. garlic powder, or 1 clove minced fresh garlic

Seasoning salt and black pepper to taste

3 cups thinly sliced unpeeled zucchini (quartered, if large)

Preheat oven to 350°. Grease a 9" x 13" pan. Mix ingredients together in order given. Place in pan. Bake for 30 – 40 minutes, until golden brown on top and firm in center. Cut into small squares to serve. Makes 24 – 48 squares, depending on how small you cut them. Freezes well.

Serves 12 – 20 as an appetizer, 4 – 6 as a main dish. This is a lot like a quiche.

Mexican 8-Layer Dip

2 cans (10 ounces each) prepared bean dip or spiced refried beans

2 avocados, peeled, seeded and chopped

1 can (4 to 9 ounces) green chilies

Mixture of 1 cup mayonnaise, 1 cup sour cream, 1 pkg. taco seasoning

1 bunch green onions, chopped

2 tomatoes, chopped

1 can (6 ounces) black olives

Starting with the bean dip, layer the ingredients in a 9" x 13" dish. Serve with tortilla chips.

Fun in the Colorado Sun

Golden, like most of Colorado, enjoys an average of 300 sunny days every year. That translates into lots of time for enjoying all of the wonderful outdoor recreation the area has to offer. Hiking the surrounding mesas and foothills has long been a popular pastime. Trails of all levels of difficulty crisscross the scenic terrain. A day hike up North or South Table Mountain affords the visitor abundant views of Denver to the east, Wyoming to the north, and Colorado Springs to the south. Rock climbing on the mesas is another favorite activity during the long summer evenings.

Greek Spinach Bake

3 eggs
2 packages (10 ounces each) frozen chopped spinach, thawed and drained well or 2 pounds fresh spinach, cooked, drained and chopped
1 package (8 ounces) feta cheese, crumbled
¼ cup chopped green onion
¼ tsp. dried dillweed

Preheat oven to 400°. Grease 2-quart shallow casserole or 12" x 8" baking dish. Beat eggs in medium size bowl until frothy. Stir in spinach, feta cheese, green onion, and dillweed. Turn into prepared casserole. Bake for 20 minutes or until knife inserted in center comes out clean. Cool on wire rack 5 minutes before serving. Serve with crackers.

Asiago Dip with Killian's Irish Red Cheese Bread

Asiago cheese is a hard cheese, like Parmesan; it's a natural accompaniment to Coors Beer, a Golden original!

Dip:

¾ cup Asiago cheese, grated

¼ cup mushrooms, sliced

¼ cup scallions, diced

2 tbsp. sun dried tomatoes, chopped

1 cup sour cream

1 cup mayonnaise

Bread:

3 cups flour

1 tbsp. baking powder

3 tbsp. sugar

½ cup cheddar cheese, grated

3 tbsp. scallions, chopped

½ tsp. ground black pepper

1 ½ cups Killian's Irish Red beer (do not use light beer)

Dip:

Reconstitute the tomatoes in hot water until pliable. Combine all ingredients in baking dish and bake at 350° until bubbly and golden brown. This dip can be prepared for a crowd in a slow cooker. Double the ingredients and cook on low heat for 2 hours. Serves 4 to 6.

Bread:

Preheat oven to 350°. Grease 4 mini bread pans. Mix together flour, baking powder and sugar. Add cheese, scallions, and pepper. Add the beer all at once, it will foam. Mix well. Divide into 4 portions. Bake for 30 minutes or until golden brown. Remove from bread pans and cool slightly. Slice thin then toast under the broiler until golden brown. Remove from oven, flip slices over and toast other side until golden. Serve with Dip. This bread is dense and very flavorful.

Fun in the Colorado Sun

Continued

The city sports a world-class kayak course on Clear Creek. Bring your own paddle because the creek doesn't take American Express! Want something a little less energetic? Try horseback riding along the hogback, or how about a stroll down our scenic creek side trail? The choice is yours; the pleasure is ours.

Spinach Artichoke Dip

16 oz. carton light sour cream
1 pkg. Good Seasons Roasted Garlic dressing mix
3 oz. pecorino-Romano cheese, grated
14 oz. artichoke hearts, drained, rinsed, and quartered
10 oz. chopped spinach (if using frozen thaw fully, drain and chop)
6 oz. mozzarella-parmesan cheese blend

Preheat oven to 400°. In a 2-qt. casserole, mix 16 ounces of sour cream, pecorino-Romano, and dressing mix. Add artichoke hearts and spinach. If you like big pieces of artichoke, stir lightly. If you like smaller pieces, stir thoroughly. Cover with remaining 7 ounces of cheese. Bake 15 minutes at 400°, then broil a few inches from broiler for 5 minutes or until golden brown.

Serve with crackers and fresh vegetable slices (baby carrots, celery, bell pepper, squash)

Fresh Asparagus and Dill Dip

½ pound fresh asparagus spears
1 cup mayonnaise
1 pint sour cream
2 tsp. dill weed
3 tsp. Spice Island brand Beau Monde seasoning

Remove woody bottoms from asparagus spears. Steam asparagus until just softened but not too limp. Chill in refrigerator. Combine the rest of the ingredients and chill as well. Serve asparagus on a nice plate with dip in bowl to the side.

Pate Beau Monde

Make this canapé spread ahead and store in freezer to have on hand for holiday entertaining.

2 packages (3 oz. each) cream cheese
1 tbsp. water
2 ½ tsp. Spice Island brand Beau Monde seasoning
¼ tsp. thyme
¼ tsp. marjoram
¼ tsp. summer savory
(in lieu of above three ingredients, you may use 1 tsp. Italian herbs)
2 tsp. parsley

Soften cream cheese with a fork. Blend in water and Beau Monde. Crush herbs and mix into cheese along with parsley. Chill for several hours for flavors to blend. Spread on crackers or fill stalks of celery.

To make a dip, omit the water and add 3 – 4 Tbsp. of light cream.

Salmon Pate

1 one-pound can salmon, drained and deboned*
1 8-oz. cream cheese, softened
2 tbsp. lemon juice
3 tsp. grated onion
1 tsp. horseradish
¼ tsp. salt
¼ tsp. Liquid Smoke

Blend all ingredients and chill. Form into a ball and roll in ½ cup chopped nuts. Make the day before to chill well. Serve with assorted crackers.
* If using smoked salmon eliminate the Liquid Smoke flavoring.

Fabulous All Purpose Dip, Salad Dressing, or Sandwich Spread

½ cup mayonnaise, light or fat-free is fine
½ cup sour cream, light or fat-free is fine
2 tbsp. chopped red onion
2 tbsp. chopped fresh dill
2 tsp. lemon juice, or to taste
Salt and pepper to taste – be generous as it mellows out
1 4-ounce can of sliced water chestnuts OR ½ cup diced cucumber OPTIONAL

Blend well and store tightly covered in refrigerator. Keeps easily for a week in refrigerator. Recipe doubles and triples well.

Chili Cheese Dip

8 oz. cream cheese
1 can (14 oz) chili with beans
1 can (4oz) diced green chilies
½ cup shredded cheddar cheese

Soften cream cheese in microwave for one minute. Add chili and green chilies. Heat for three minutes on medium power. Stir. Dip should be very smooth and easy to scoop with a chip. Heat longer, if necessary. Top with cheese and return to microwave for another 45 – 60 seconds, until cheese is melted. Serve hot, with tortilla chips.

Crab Mousse

1 10-oz. can cream of mushroom soup
1 8 oz. cream cheese
1 envelope unflavored gelatin
¼ cup cold water
½ cup finely chopped celery
½ cup finely chopped green onions
1 cup mayonnaise
½ - ¾ lb. crabmeat
¼ tsp. curry powder

Heat together soup and cream cheese, stirring until smooth. Add gelatin to cold water and soften 5 minutes. Add to soup mixture and stir to dissolve. Add remaining ingredients. Mix well. Pour into a 4 cup mold and chill overnight. Unmold, garnish and serve with crackers. Serves a crowd.

Shrimp Dip

2 small cans (4 ½ oz.) tiny cleaned shrimp
1 8 oz. pkg. cream cheese or Neufchatel
½ cup mayonnaise (light mayo is fine)
Chili sauce to taste
2 tsp. horseradish or to taste

Soften cream cheese. Mix softened cream cheese, mayo, horseradish, and some chili sauce until it's about the color of shrimp but not too runny. Rinse the shrimp in cold water and drain well. Break up or mash the shrimp. Add to other ingredients. Taste and add more horseradish and chili sauce if desired.

Serves a crowd. Great on pumpernickel bread or crackers. Can cut recipe in half for a smaller crowd.

Braunschweiger Pate

1 lb. Braunschweiger (in a tube)
1 8 oz. package cream cheese
2 tbsp. lemon juice
1 package dry onion soup mix
2 tbsp. Worcestershire
1 tbsp. horseradish
Dash Tabasco sauce
Chopped pecans

Bring Braunschweiger and cream cheese to room temperature before mixing. In a food processor or large mixer bowl, blend Braunschweiger and cream cheese. Add remaining ingredients and mix well. Shape into a log, wrap in plastic. Chill overnight, or even a day or two longer to blend flavors. Sprinkle top with chopped pecans before serving. Serve with crackers or rye bread rounds.

Kahlua Dip

8 oz. cream cheese
8 oz. Cool Whip
¾ cup brown sugar
1 cup sour cream
1/3 cup Kahlua

Mix ingredients.

Use as a dip for fresh cut fruit.

Asian Dipping Sauce

Great for all tempura, dim sum, gyoza, etc.

4 tbsp. soy sauce
2 tbsp. red wine vinegar
½ tsp. sesame oil
¼ tsp. fresh minced garlic
¼ tsp. fresh minced ginger

Blend all ingredients, store in refrigerator. To reduce the saltiness of the sauce, add ½ tsp. sugar or honey.

Indonesian Peanut Sauce (Bumbu Katjang)

1/3 cup smooth peanut butter
1/3 cup water
¼ cup canned cream of coconut
¼ cup lemon juice
1 ¼ tsp. Indonesian red pepper sauce
½ tsp. salt
1 split clove garlic
1" square lemon peel

Cook over low heat in a small pan, whisking until smooth. Remove garlic and serve warm. Ideal to serve over sate or chicken breasts.

Sauce can be found in Asian markets OR 1 tsp Tabasco sauce can be used in place of Indonesian red pepper sauce.

Goat Cheese Quesadillas with Mango Salsa

4 ounces of mushrooms: shiitake, crimini, oyster or a mixture, sliced
4 ounces canned black beans, drained and mashed
¼ cup red bell pepper, julienned
2 tbsp. olive oil
1 tsp. garlic, minced
2 tbsp. green onions, sliced
7 ounces goat cheese, crumbled
6 flour tortillas
Mango salsa (recipe below)
Guacamole

Over high heat, sauté the mushrooms and bell pepper in olive oil for about 4 minutes. Add the garlic and green onions, sauté 2 minutes more. Add in the mashed black beans and heat just until beans are warmed through. Remove from heat, stir in goat cheese.

Spread 3 tbsp. of mixture onto 3 tortillas, top with remaining 3 tortillas. Grill each side of quesadilla in a large flat skillet or a Comal just until golden brown. Cut into wedges and serve with mango salsa and guacamole. Serves six.

Mango Salsa

1 jalapeno, seeded and diced
1 mango, peeled and sliced from seed
¼ cup red onion, diced
1 tsp. lemon juice
1/8 tsp. salt

Combine ingredients in non-reactive bowl. Chill, if not using immediately. Bring up to room temperature for serving.

Reuben Dip

This is fast becoming a favorite with the volunteers at the Golden Visitors Center during the Olde Golden Christmas Celebration

1 – (3-ounce) package cream cheese
¼ cup sour cream
4 ounces sliced corned beef finely chopped
½ cup grated Swiss cheese
¼ cup sauerkraut, drained and chopped
2 – 3 tbsp. milk

Heat cream cheese, sour cream, corned beef, Swiss cheese and sauerkraut in a small pan over low heat until hot, thin with milk if necessary. Serve with rye crackers or cocktail rye bread.

This dip goes really fast so you might want to double or triple the recipe!

Mock Margaritas

6 ounces lemonade concentrate
6 ounces limeade concentrate
3 cups crushed ice
½ cup powdered sugar

   Mix well and freeze. When ready to serve, place mixture in blender with 3 cups club soda. Blend until well mixed. Dip rims of glasses in salt, and serve cold.

Moonlight Margarita

   A good summer drink.

6 ounces gold tequila
1 ounce blue Curacao
4 ounces Triple Sec
4 ounces lime juice

   In a blender, combine 2 cups crushed ice with ingredients. Serve in clear glass tumblers. Serves 4.

Mountain Melter

2 ounces gold tequila
1 ounce Triple Sec
dash cinnamon schnapps
8 ounces hot chocolate

   Divide ingredients between two large mugs. Serves 2.

Perfect Punch

1 cup sugar
2 ¾ cups water
2 ripe bananas, sliced
3 cups unsweetened pineapple juice
6 ounces orange juice concentrate
2 tbsp. lemon juice
1 liter lemon-lime soda

Combine water and sugar until sugar dissolves. In a blender or food processor place bananas, half of pineapple juice and orange juice concentrate. Process until smooth. Combine with remaining juice and sugar water. Pour into freezer-safe container and freeze for at least 4 hours.

To serve: Remove from freezer at least 30 minutes before serving. Allow to thaw slightly for 30 minutes. Scrape frozen mixture into punch bowl. Pour lemon-lime soda down the side of the punch bowl. Serves 24.

Spiced Punch

1/3 cup sugar
½ cup water
6 cinnamon sticks, broken
½ tsp. whole cloves
4 cups apple juice, chilled
12 ounces apricot nectar, chilled
¼ cup lemon juice
Two 750-ml. Bottles Chardonnay, chilled

In a saucepan, combine water, sugar, and spices. Bring to boil; reduce heat. Cover and simmer 10 minutes. Chill at least 2 hours in a covered container.

Strain spices from sugar water and discard. Combine with juices and pour into punch bowl. Add wine. Serves 24.

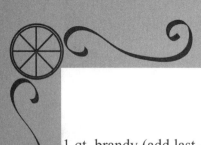

Brandy Slush

1 qt. brandy (add last - when lukewarm)
1 12 oz. can frozen orange juice
1 12 oz. can frozen lemonade
7 cups water, bring to a boil and add 2 cups sugar
2 cups boiling water, 4 tea bags (steep)

Mix above ingredients together. Let cool to lukewarm. Freeze for 12 hours to a slush. When mixture is slush, scoop a portion into a glass. Pour 7Up or black cherry soda over top.

Tea Tropicale

6 cups boiling water
12 tea bags
1 cup granulated sugar
2/3 cup Minute Maid 100% pure lemon juice
1 cup orange juice
1 quart chilled ginger ale
sprigs of mint

Pour boiling water over tea bags and let stand 5 minutes; remove bags. Add sugar and stir till dissolved. Add fruit juices. Pour into pitcher half full of ice. Just before serving, slowly pour ginger ale down side of pitcher. Decorate with mint. Makes about 12 servings.

Hot Punch

1 qt. apple cider or juice
1 pint cranberry juice
1 cup orange juice
¾ cup lemon juice
1 cup sugar
1 tsp. allspice
1 tsp. cloves
3 cinnamon sticks

Put juice in bottom of percolator, sugar and spice on top and perk.

Cinnamon Mulling Spice

1 lemon
15 cinnamon sticks, 3 inches each
1 ½ tbsp. whole cloves
1 ½ tbsp. whole allspice
2 tsp. whole anise seed, crushed

With a sharp paring knife, cut a thin strip of lemon peel about 1/4 inch wide, beginning at one end of lemon. Place peel on baking sheet. Bake in preheated 225° oven about one hour or until dry. Cut into 1/4 inch pieces. Place a few cinnamon sticks at a time in a plastic bag. Crush into slivers (about 1 inch) using a rolling pin or heavy mallet. Repeat with remaining cinnamon. Mix cinnamon, cloves, allspice, anise and lemon peel. Place 3 tbsp. of the mixture in center of a 5 inch square of cheesecloth or muslin. Bring corners together. Tie with string to make a bag. Repeat. Use to flavor red wine, fruit juices, such as apple and cranberry, tea or poached fruit. Place one bag in one quart of liquid in non-aluminum pan. Simmer, covered 15 or 20 minutes, depending on the flavoring strength desired. Serve warm. Makes 8 spice bags or 2 cups spice mixture.

Purple Mountain Majesty Margarita

Coarse sugar
4 ounces silver tequila
1 ounce Triple Sec
6 ounces margarita mix
2 ounces black raspberry liqueur, such as Chambord
lime slices

Dip rims of glasses in a bowl of water, then in a bowl of coarse sugar. Combine tequila, Triple Sec, and margarita mix in a pitcher, mix well. Pour mixture over ice in margarita glasses. Float a ½ ounce of black raspberry liqueur on top of each glass. Garnish with a lime slice on the rim.

To make frozen: combine all ingredients in a blender with 3 cups of crushed ice. Blend and pour into glasses.

Red, White & Blueberry Smoothies

6 milk cubes (recipe below)
1 cup low-fat blueberry yogurt
1 cup sliced strawberries
1 cup 1% milk
2 tbsp. honey

To make milk cubes, pour no fat milk into ice cube trays; freeze. Remove cubes from trays. Store in a plastic freezer bag or covered freezer container.

For the smoothies, combine six milk cubes and the remaining ingredients in a blender. Blend on high until smooth. Pour mixture into four tall glasses. For ice pops, pour mixture into pop molds and freeze, or fill ice cube trays, cover tightly with plastic wrap, stick a toothpick into each cube and freeze. Makes four 8-ounce smoothies or 30 ice cube tray pops.

Hot or Hot-Buttered Lemonade

Grated peel of ½ lemon
½ cup lemon juice
3 cups water
½ cup sugar
¼ cup light rum (optional)
1 tbsp. butter (optional)

   Combine all ingredients in saucepan. Heat. Makes about 4 cups (five 6-ounce servings).

Rose Punch

2 packages (16 ounces) frozen sliced strawberries, partly thawed
½ cup sugar
½ gallon rose wine
2 cans (6 ounces each) frozen lemonade concentrate
1 quart soda water, chilled
Ice ring or 1 tray ice cubes

   Put berries in large bowl. Stir in sugar and half the wine. Cover and let stand at room temperature 1 hour. Force mixture through fine sieve. Return to bowl. Add frozen lemonade. Stir until thawed. Add remaining wine, soda water, and ice. Stir to blend. Serve at once in punch cups or wine glasses. Makes 3 ½ quarts.

Hot Mulled Wine

This is great after skiing or even just shoveling snow. Guaranteed to warm you up!

3 tea bags

1 ½ cups red wine

½ cup light brown sugar

stick cinnamon (optional)

lemon slices (optional)

raisins (optional)

almonds (optional)

Bring one quart of water to boil and add tea bags. Remove from heat; steep covered for 5 minutes. Discard tea bags. Add wine and brown sugar. Stir until sugar is dissolved. Add whatever optional ingredients are available and sound good. Reheat for an additional 2 minutes at high in microwave. Strain if desired. Serve in mugs.

You can vary the taste by using different kinds of tea, such as Orange Spice or Cranberry.

Pioneer Sangria

Museums traditionally don't permit red beverages anywhere near the building. To enjoy this sangria the Golden Pioneer Museum holds outdoor celebrations on our patio overlooking Clear Creek.

4 large oranges

2 large lemons

2 limes

½ cup superfine sugar

½ cup Triple Sec

1 gallon inexpensive Merlot, chilled

Wash oranges, lemons, and limes. Slice 2 oranges, 2 lemons, and 2 limes into thin slices. Separate slices of each citrus into 2 large pitchers. Pour ¼ cup sugar into each pitcher; mash slices with wooden spoon until slightly pulpy and sugar is dissolved. Juice remaining 2 oranges. Divide orange juice, Triple Sec, and wine between pitchers. Stir gently. Refrigerate for at least 4 hours. Before serving, stir up pulp and fruit slices. Looks beautiful served in a clear glass punchbowl.

Snow Ball

1 ounce coffee flavored brandy
1 ounce cinnamon schnapps
12 ounces hot coffee

Divide ingredients between 2 mugs. Garnish with whipped cream.

A Warm Cozy Fire

2 ounces brandy cream
2 ounces butterscotch schnapps
8 ounces hot chocolate

Divide ingredients into 2 large mugs. Top with a dollop of whipped cream and cozy up for a long winter's night.

Wassail: Christmas Drink

A salutation or toast given in drinking someone's health or as an expression of good will at a festivity. The drink used in such toasting, commonly ale or wine spiced with roasted apples and sugar.

1 gallon apple cider
2 quarts orange juice
1 cup granulated sugar
½ tsp. salt
3 cinnamon sticks
½ tsp. whole cloves

Mix all ingredients in a large pot. (A stock pot or large pasta pot works well.) Simmer over low heat for three hours. Stir occasionally. Strain and serve hot. A cinnamon stick served in the cup adds a festive touch.

Strawberry Sparkle Punch

2 cups fresh or frozen strawberries, hulled
1 3-ounce package strawberry Jell-O
1 cup boiling water
1 6-ounce can frozen lemonade

3 cups cold water
1 1-quart bottle cranberry juice cocktail, chilled
1 12-ounce bottle ginger ale, chilled

In a blender, puree strawberries. In a large bowl, dissolve Jell-O in boiling water. Stir in lemonade concentrate until melted. Add cold water, cranberry juice cocktail, and strawberry puree. Pour over ice in a large punch bowl. Slowly add ginger ale.

Serves 25-30

Colorado Sunset Smoothie

There's a saying in these parts: If God's not a Bronco fan, then why are sunsets orange? This drink reflects some of the beauty of those fabulous Colorado sunsets.

1 ½ cups orange juice
2 tbsp. whole berry cranberry sauce
1 cup vanilla yogurt

In a blender, process all ingredients on medium speed until smooth.

Rock n' Raspberry Smoothie

1 cup red raspberries, fresh or frozen
½ cup apple juice, more if you want a thinner drink
1 cup low-fat plain or red raspberry yogurt
¼ cup All-Fruit raspberry jam
½ cup frozen vanilla yogurt
2 ice cubes

Combine all ingredients in a blender until smooth. Strain if desired.

From The Hearth

Mining was crucial to Golden's early economic development. While gold mines were rare in the town, coal was king. Gold ore must be smelted to extract the precious mineral from the surrounding rock; Golden had several coal mines, including the White Ash that supplied the town's smelters with coal for the process. Clay had been mined in Golden, as well. For 125 years, the Parfet family provided fine buff clay for bricks throughout the region, ceasing mining operations in 2003. Visitors can view the remnants of Golden's mining operations in several locations, including the new Fossil Trace Golf Course which is constructed over an old clay mine, and at the White Ash Memorial marker.

(Photo: White Ash miners, c.1885; courtesy of the Golden Pioneer Museum)

Lemon Cream Scones

2 cups unbleached flour
1/3 cup sugar
1 tbsp. baking powder
¼ tsp. salt
½ cup golden raisins

1 tsp. finely grated lemon peel
1 cup whipping cream
3 tbsp. lemon juice
1 egg, beaten

Preheat oven to 375°. In a large bowl, mix together flour, sugar, baking powder and salt. Stir in raisins and lemon zest. Slowly stir in cream and lemon juice. Stir just until dough is formed. Turn dough out onto a lightly floured board and knead dough for a minute. Pat dough into an 8-inch circle and cut out scones with a 2-inch biscuit cutter. Place circles on a greased baking sheet; brush tops with beaten egg. Bake 25-30 minutes or until golden brown.

Apricot Sour Cream Scones

4 cups flour
½ cup sugar
4 tsp. baking powder
2 tsp. salt
½ tsp. cream of tartar
¾ cup butter, well-chilled
    (not margarine)
2 tbsp. grated orange peel

1 cup chopped dried apricots
1 egg
½ cup sour cream
½ cup whipping cream
½ cup orange juice
additional cream
Demara or large crystal sugar

Preheat oven to 425°.   In a large bowl, combine flour, sugar, baking powder, salt, and cream of tartar. Cut in butter until mixture resembles coarse crumbs. Add orange peel and apricots. In a separate bowl combine egg, sour cream, whipping cream, and orange juice. Add to dry ingredients and mix lightly until soft dough forms; it will be sticky. Turn the dough onto lightly floured surface and knead 5 to 6 times. Pat into ½ thick circle and cut into wedges. Place onto lightly greased baking sheet, brush with additional cream and sprinkle with Demara sugar. Bake for 20 minutes or until golden.

Gingerbread Raisin Scones

2 cups all purpose flour
1/3 cup packed brown sugar
1 tbsp. baking powder
¾ tsp. ground cinnamon
½ tsp. ground ginger
1/8 tsp. ground cloves
6 tbsp. (3/4 stick) butter, chilled and cut into pieces
¼ cup milk
1 large egg
3 tbsp. light unsulphured molasses

Preheat oven to 375º.   Lightly grease baking sheet. Blend first 6 ingredients in food processor. Add butter and process until mixture resembles coarse meal. In a separate bowl, beat together milk, egg, molasses, and vanilla in a large bowl until blended. Add in flour and raisins. Stir gently until dough forms. Gather dough into ball. On a lightly floured surface, press dough into 1" thick round. Cut round into 8 wedges. Place on baking sheet. Bake 25 minutes or until golden brown.

Mini Tea Muffins

1/3 cup poppy seeds
1 cup milk
3 tsp. baking powder
½ tsp. salt
2 cups flour
½ tsp. nutmeg

zest of one lemon
½ cup sugar
1 egg, slightly beaten
3 tbsp. butter, melted and cooled
1 cup frozen blueberries

Lightly grease 24 mini-muffin cups or use paper liners. Soak the poppy seeds in the milk for 30 minutes. Combine the flour, sugar, baking powder, salt, nutmeg, and lemon zest. Add the poppy seed mixture, egg, and melted butter. Stir just until the ingredients are moistened. Carefully stir in the blueberries. Spoon the batter into the prepared muffin tins, filling 2/3 full. Bake in a preheated 375° oven for 15 – 20 minutes. Turn onto a wire rack and cool. Makes 24 muffins.

Chocolate Chocolate Chip Muffins

These muffins are wonderfully rich and chocolate-y. Use the best quality chocolate you can to achieve the ultimate in flavor.

1 stick butter or margarine
3 squares unsweetened chocolate
1 cup sugar
1 egg
2 tsp. pure vanilla extract

dash of salt
1 cup buttermilk
2 cups all purpose flour
1 tsp. baking soda
1 cup chocolate chips

Preheat oven to 400°. Melt butter or margarine and unsweetened chocolate (use a double boiler or can be done in microwave). Set aside. In large mixer bowl, add sugar, egg, vanilla, and salt. Mix until blended. Add buttermilk, flour, and baking soda. Pour chocolate/butter or margarine mix on top of flour mixture. Mix. Add chocolate chips and mix again. Pour batter into lined or lightly greased muffin tins. Any size muffin tin may be used. Number of muffins will vary depending upon size of pan. Bake for 15 – 20 minutes. Yields 18 traditional size muffins.

Plum Bread

This recipe is from an old friend of the family who operates a vineyard and Bed & Breakfast in Sperryville, Virginia. Marilyn makes this bread during the holidays and it is always popular.

3 eggs
2 cups sugar
1 cup oil
2 small jars of baby food plums
2 tsp. baking soda
1 cup buttermilk
5 cups flour
2 tsp. baking soda
1 tsp. cinnamon
¼ tsp. cloves
1 tsp. salt
1 cup chopped pecans

Mix the first 4 ingredients. In a separate bowl, mix baking soda in buttermilk and set aside. Combine flour with cinnamon, cloves and salt. Add flour and milk mixtures alternately to egg and sugar mixture. Stir in chopped pecans. Blend thoroughly. Bake 1 hour at 325°. Makes 5 small pans or 2 8" loaf pans.

Rocky Mountain Quilt Museum

1111 Washington Avenue
Golden, CO 80401
303.277.0377
www.rmqm.org

One of only a few museums in the United States dedicated to the art of quilting, the Rocky Mountain Quilt Museum welcomes visitors from all over the world. Its mission is to enrich the lives of people of all ages, backgrounds, and cultures through the celebration of, education about and preservation of quilts and quilt making, past and present. In 1990, the museum opened its doors with an initial collection of 100 quilts donated by its founder Eugenia Mitchell. The museum now boasts a collection of over 250 quilts.

Peanut Butter Bread

2 cups flour
3 tsp. baking powder
1/3 cup sugar
¼ cup dry milk
¼ tsp. salt
½ cup peanut butter
1½ cups skim milk

Preheat oven to 350°. Sift together flour, baking powder, sugar, dry milk, and salt. Cut in peanut butter until mixture resembles coarse crumbs. Add skim milk and mix, then beat with a few quick strokes. Pour into oiled and floured 4" x 8" loaf pan. Bake about one hour or until wooden toothpick comes out clean. Serves 16.

Poppy Seed Bread

4 eggs beaten   1 cup chopped nuts
1½ cups vegetable oil   3 cups flour
1½ tsp. baking soda   ½ tsp. salt
2 cups sugar   2 ounces poppy seeds
12 ounce can evaporated milk

Preheat oven to 350°. Mix all ingredients together and pour into a greased 10" tube pan or two loaf pans. Bake for one hour and fifteen minutes. Let cool 20 – 30 minutes before removing from pan.

Zucchini Bread

2 cups grated zucchini
3 eggs
1½ cups sugar
½ cup vegetable oil
3 cups flour
1 tsp. baking soda

1½ tsp. baking powder
3 tsp. cinnamon
1 tsp. salt
1 tsp. vanilla
½ cup chopped nuts

Preheat oven to 350°. Grease and flour (very well) a medium loaf pan. Mix together all ingredients in a large bowl. Bake 40 – 50 minutes in preheated oven.

Date and Nut Bread

2 cups pitted dates
1½ cups boiling water
1½ cups sugar
1 tsp. vegetable oil
1 tsp. vanilla
1 egg

2¾ cups sifted all purpose (or high-altitude) flour
1 cup chopped, toasted pecans
½ tsp. salt
2 tsp. baking soda

Preheat oven to 350°. Combine dates with boiling water; set aside. Combine sugar, oil, vanilla, and egg. Blend until creamy. Fold in dates with water and blend. Fold in flour, pecans, salt and baking powder. Bake in 2 well-greased loaf pans for one hour. Test for doneness with a toothpick inserted in center of loaf; when toothpick comes out clean, bread is done. Allow to cool before serving or freezing.

For lower cholesterol version, use 2 egg whites and no yolks.

Rocky Mountain Quilt Museum

Continued

Visitors enjoy 5 changing exhibits in its two exhibition galleries. Both traditional and contemporary quilts are shown. Adult and children's quilting classes are provided in both machine and hand techniques. The museum is home to the QuiltMarket, a unique gift shop offering new and vintage quilts and a wide selection of quilt-related gifts and books. The museum is located beneath Golden's famous arch and is open Monday - Saturday, 10:00am - 4:00pm.

Tips for Successful Prospecting

In its early years, Golden thrived because of its proximity to the mountain gold mining towns. Gold prospectors coming from the East who had no survival skills for the frontier, just a desire to get rich quick, were called "green horns." There was a lot to learn for these inexperienced adventurers. Gold is still floating just beneath the surface of Clear Creek - try your luck today!

If using a gold pan for cooking, wash with soap and rinse thoroughly, as the grease will allow fine gold to float off.

Double Quick Rolls

1 package dry yeast
1 cup water
2 tbsp. sugar
2¼ cups flour
1 tsp. salt
1 egg
2 tbsp. softened shortening

Dissolve yeast in water. Stir in sugar, 1 cup flour, and salt. Add egg and shortening. Beat in remaining flour until smooth. Cover with cloth and let rise in warm place until double in bulk; about 30 minutes.

Grease 12 large muffin cups. Stir down raised dough. Spoon into muffin cups, filling ½ full. Let rise in warm place until dough reaches top of cups; 20-30 minutes. Bake at 400° for 15 – 20 minutes.

Jalapeno Cornbread

This is the perfect accompaniment to a hearty bowl of soup or chili.

3 cups cornbread mix
2½ cups milk
½ cup oil
3 eggs, beaten
1 large onion, grated
2 tbsp. sugar
½ tsp. garlic powder
1 cup cream style corn
¼ to ½ tsp. jalapeno peppers, chopped
1½ cup cheddar cheese, grated
4 pieces bacon, fried, drained, and crumbled
1 small jar chopped pimentos

Preheat oven to 425°. Mix ingredients in a large bowl. Grease a 9" x 12" pan and heat in oven. Pour mixture into warm pan. Bake 45 minutes.

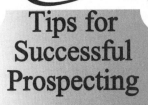

Tips for Successful Prospecting

Continued

When using a sluice box, Long Tom, or rocker, do not allow minerals to overload the riffles, as the fine gold may be lost downstream.

Geologic conditions marking a successful mine in one area might not mark a successful mine in another area.

Gold veins become more expensive to work the deeper you go.

Placer (pan) deposits usually return a good value when named after a woman. Doesn't matter which one, any woman will do.

Mexican Spoon Bread

1 cup yellow cornmeal
1 tsp. salt
½ tsp. baking soda
¾ cup milk
¼ cup oil
2 eggs, beaten
1 can (16 oz.) cream style corn

1 can (4 oz.) green chilies, drained
1½ cups shredded sharp Cheddar cheese
    OR Cheddar-Monterey Jack mixture

Preheat oven to 350°. Combine cornmeal, salt, and baking soda. Add milk and oil. Mix well. Add beaten eggs, cream style corn and mix thoroughly. Spoon into greased 1½ quart casserole dish. Sprinkle with ½ of the green chilies and ½ of the cheese. Repeat layers. Bake for 40 – 45 minutes.

Quick Cinnamon Rolls

These rich rolls have more of a biscuit consistency than that of a traditional roll. Use as much cinnamon and cloves as suit your personal taste.

4 cups flour	1 1/3 cup milk
6 tsp. baking powder	margarine
¼ tsp. salt	brown sugar
4 tbsp. sugar	cinnamon
2/3 cup oil	ground cloves

Preheat oven to 475°. Stir together flour, baking powder, sugar, and salt. Pour in oil and milk all at once. Mix lightly with fork until mixture comes away from side of the bowl. Turn out on floured board and knead enough to make ball. Pat out with fingers to make rectanglular piece about ½" thick, 9" x 15". Spread top with soft margarine. Sprinkle on brown sugar to cover. Sprinkle on cinnamon to taste. Sprinkle on ground cloves lightly. Roll up to make long roll, with seam at bottom. Use hands to even out roll and tuck in ends. Cut into 1 ¼" pieces. Place cut side up on baking sheet. Leave at least 1" between each slice. Bake until lightly brown, about 10 minutes. Remove from sheet. Makes 15 rolls. While still warm, frost with powdered sugar icing.

Powdered Sugar Icing

2 tbsp. margarine, softened
2 tbsp. canned milk or cream
enough powdered sugar to make medium thick frosting

Mix margarine and some sugar; add milk. Add more sugar gradually until desired consistency is reached.

Golden Landmarks Association

Continued

Golden Landmarks Association is involved in many preservation and education efforts. GLA has a large collection of historic photographs and artifacts and is creating a library of oral histories of some of the citizens who have played a role in the shaping of Golden. Each year, GLA honors those that have made significant contributions to preserving Golden's history with the Living Landmarks Awards.

Golden Landmarks Association: preserving our past, protecting our future.

Clotted Cream

This is a lovely addition to any scone and a complement to any preserves served.

1 cup heavy cream, at room temperature
1/3 cup sour cream, at room temperature
1 tbsp. confectioner's sugar

One hour before serving, pour the heavy cream into a bowl and whip until soft peaks form. Whisk in the sour cream and sugar, continuing to beat until the mixture is very thick. Chill until ready to serve.

If you want to make this ahead of time, it will last about 4 to 6 hours in the refrigerator. Serves 4 - 6

Basic Scones

2 cups flour
2½ tsp. baking powder
¼ tsp. salt
4 tbsp. butter
¾ cup milk

Sift dry ingredients together. Cut in butter until crumbly. Add milk and blend well; dough will be sticky. Flour a flat work space and knead the dough for about half a minute. Roll out ½ inch thick and cut into whatever shape you like (triangles are traditional). Bake at 400° for about 15 minutes.

Makes about 12 scones, depending on size.

Note: There are scores of scone variations. You can add dried fruit, nuts, or chocolate chips (about one cup). For slightly sweeter scones, add ¼ cup sugar. For richness, use cream instead of milk. You can also add 1 egg (decrease milk to ½ cup) or increase the amount of butter for richer texture.

Sausage Soufflé

1 lb. sausage links, cut in bite size pieces, browned and (drained*)
8 slices of white bread, crusts removed and cubed
2 cups grated sharp cheddar cheese
4 eggs, beaten
2½ cups milk
¾ tsp. dry mustard

Grease a 9" x 13" baking pan. Place bread cubes in bottom of pan. Sprinkle grated cheese and then sausage bits on top of bread cubes. Beat together the eggs, milk, and mustard and pour over cheese and sausage. Refrigerate overnight.

1 can cream of mushroom soup
½ cup milk

In the morning, preheat oven to 300°. Blend soup and milk and pour over casserole. Place pan in oven uncovered and bake for 1½ hours.

*Ham or shrimp may be substituted for sausage.

Never Fail Cheese Soufflé

8 slices of white bread
1 cup shredded cheddar cheese
1 cup shredded mozzarella cheese
8 eggs, beaten until foamy
3½ cups half and half

6 slices of fresh onion
1 1-lb. cooked and crumbled sausage
   or Italian sausage
1/8 tsp each salt and pepper

Butter sides and bottom of 9" x 13" baking dish. Cut away bread crusts. Butter each slice and cut into cubes. Place half of butter cubes in baking dish. Top with half of cheese and sausage. Add remaining bread and top with remaining cheese and sausage. Combine eggs, half and half, salt and pepper. Pour over bread. Top with sliced onion rings. Cover and refrigerate overnight. Bake at 325° for one hour or until top is lightly browned. Note: This is also very good without meat.

Bulgarian Potato & Sausage Casserole

3 cups cottage cheese
1 stick butter, melted
2 tsp. salt
1 tsp. pepper
½ onion, chopped
6 large potatoes, peeled and sliced

1 lb. sausage, cooked and diced
2 cups cheddar cheese
4 eggs
2 cups sour cream
1 tbsp. chives

Preheat oven to 375°. Grease a 9" x 13" pan. Mix cottage cheese, butter, salt, cheddar cheese, pepper, and onion. Layer casserole with potato slices, sausage and cheese mixture ending with a cheese layer. Bake at 375° for 30 minutes. Beat eggs with sour cream and chives. Spread over casserole. Bake another 35 – 45 minutes or until topping is puffed and golden brown and potatoes test tender with fork. If you pre-cook your potatoes you can reduce total cooking time to 45 – 55 minutes.

South Table Strata

A satisfying, easy dish that's also versatile: Accompany with sliced melon and some assorted pastries for brunch, or with a green salad and warm focaccia for dinner.

1 lb. mild Italian sausage, casings removed
½ cup chopped shallots
2 garlic cloves, minced
½ cup oil-packed sun-dried tomatoes, chopped and drained
4 tbsp. chopped fresh parsley
5 large eggs
3 large egg yolks
1 cup half and half
1 cup whipping cream
2 cups grated mozzarella
½ tsp. salt

Preheat oven to 375°F. Butter a 13"x9"x2"glass baking dish. Sauté sausage in medium nonstick skillet over medium heat, breaking up with back of fork into small pieces, about 10 minutes or until brown and cooked through. Add shallots and garlic and sauté 3 minutes. Add sun-dried tomatoes and 2 tablespoons parsley; stir 1 minute. Spread sausage mixture in prepared dish. (Can be made one day ahead. Cover and refrigerate.)

Whisk eggs, egg yolks, half and half, whipping cream, 1½ cups cheese, and salt in large bowl to blend well. Pour egg mixture over sausage mixture in dish. Sprinkle remaining ½ cup cheese and 2 tablespoons parsley over top. Bake until top of casserole is golden brown and knife inserted into center comes out clean, about 30 minutes. Let stand 5 minutes before serving.

Serves 8

Colorado Quiche

2 cups onion, thinly sliced
1 tbsp. butter
1 9" unbaked pie shell
½ lb. grated Swiss cheese
3 eggs
2/3 cup half and half
1 tsp. salt
¼ tsp. pepper

Sauté onion in butter until soft and golden in color. Layer in pie shell alternating with grated Swiss cheese. Combine eggs with half and half, salt and pepper. Beat lightly and pour over filling. Bake at 400° 30 minutes. Test with knife – should be like custard. Let stand 10 minutes before serving.

A fool-proof recipe. Quiche is my choice when having guests for brunch or lunch. I always use Pillsbury refrigerated crust. It's the best. I sometimes add extra eggs and use canned milk instead of half and half. You can add broccoli or spinach, chunks of ham or crumble bacon. I even have substituted different kinds of cheese. You can't ruin it. It's always good.

Onion Pie

2 onions, sliced
10 strips bacon
4 eggs
2 cups milk

3 tbsp. flour
1 cup Parmesan cheese
salt, nutmeg, white pepper to taste
2 unbaked 9-inch pie shells

Sauté bacon and onion slices together. Drain off half of drippings. In a large bowl, beat eggs and milk together. Sprinkle flour in with bacon and onion, then add seasonings. Mix in egg mixture. Divide cheese and sprinkle over bottom of pie shells, pour in filling. Sprinkle top with remaining cheese. Bake at 350° for about 45 minutes or until knife inserted in the center comes out clean.

Blueberry French Toast

12 slices of bread, cubed
8 ounces cream cheese
1 cup fresh or frozen blueberries
12 eggs
2 cups milk
½ cup maple syrup

Put half of the bread cubes in a greased 9" x 13" baking dish. Cube the cream cheese and sprinkle it over the bread. Distribute blueberries evenly over the bread cubes and cream cheese. Add the remaining bread cubes. Combine the eggs, milk and syrup. Mix together well and pour over the bread cube mixture. Cover with foil and refrigerate overnight.

In the morning, preheat oven to 350°. Bake the dish, covered, for 30 minutes. Uncover and bake another 30 minutes or until set. Serve warm with warm syrup of your choice.

Serves 12

Stuffed French Toast

5 – 6 slices raisin bread, cubed
2 8oz. packages cream cheese
5 – 6 slices sourdough bread, cubed
12 eggs
2 cups milk
½ cup maple or pancake syrup
    or a combination of syrups
vanilla extract to taste
dash salt
Berry Topping (recipe follows)

Spray a 9" x 13" glass baking dish with cooking spray. Place a thick layer of raisin bread cubes on the bottom. Slice the cream cheese and place on top of the bread. Add cubed sourdough on top of the cream cheese.

In a large bowl mix the remaining ingredients and pour over the bread. Cover and refrigerate overnight.

Bake uncovered in a 350° oven for about 45 – 50 minutes or until done. Top each serving with Berry Topping.

Berry Topping:

In a saucepan heat a large can of partially thawed frozen strawberries in syrup. Add a cup or two of frozen mixed berries as well. Spoon over individual squares of French Toast. Top with a dollop of sour cream and a "snowfall" of confectioners' sugar.

Makes 6 – 8 servings

Pumpkin Pancakes

Great on a crisp fall morning!

2 cups biscuit mix
2 tbsp. packed light brown sugar
2 tsp. ground cinnamon
1 tsp. ground allspice
1½ cups undiluted evaporated milk

½ cup pumpkin pureé
2 tbsp. vegetable oil
2 eggs
1 tsp. pure vanilla extract

In a large mixer bowl, combine biscuit mix, sugar, cinnamon, and allspice. Add evaporated milk, pumpkin, oil, eggs, and vanilla. Beat until smooth. Pour ¼ to ½ cup batter (depending on size of pancake desired) onto heated and lightly greased griddle. Cook until top surface is bubbly and edges are dry. Turn, cook until golden. Keep pancakes warm in a 200° oven.

Serve with maple syrup or honey.

Makes about 16 pancakes.

Wild About Bananas Pancakes

1 cup flour
2 tbsp. sugar
1 tsp. baking powder
½ tsp. baking soda
2 very ripe bananas, mashed
½ tsp. salt

2 tbsp. vegetable oil
1 cup buttermilk
1 egg
1 cup walnuts, chopped
½ tsp. vanilla

Combine all ingredients in a mixing bowl. Beat on low until no lumps remain. Thin with skim milk if it seems too thick. Cook on a hot griddle until golden brown.

Apple Pancakes

1 cup sifted flour
1 tbsp. sugar
¼ tsp. salt
2 eggs, beaten
1 cup milk

8 tbsp. butter
3 tart, firm apples, peeled and sliced
cinnamon-sugar mixture
powdered sugar

In a bowl, combine flour, sugar, and salt. Make a well and add eggs and milk. Beat until smooth. Let stand. Place 3 tablespoons of the butter into a skillet and sauté apples until golden and tender. Remove and sprinkle with cinnamon-sugar. Keep warm in 200° oven.

In a pan, melt some of the remaining butter. Add the batter for one pancake at a time, tilt pan to spread batter evenly. Cook until lightly browned on one side and then turn over. Repeat for each pancake. When finished, put some apple mixture on each, roll up. Sprinkle tops of rolled pancakes with powdered sugar.

Vasquez Forks Waffles

These waffles are a bit labor intensive, but well worth the effort because they are very fluffy.

2 cups flour
¼ tsp. salt
2 tsp. baking powder
3 eggs, separated
2 cups sour milk
6 tbsp. butter, melted

In a large bowl, beat egg yolks until light yellow and frothy. Add one cup of sour milk. Sift together dry ingredients, add to egg yolk mixture and beat. Add remaining milk and melted butter. In a separate bowl, beat egg whites until stiff peaks form, fold into batter. Bake on hot waffle iron to desired level of doneness. Serves 6

Ginger Pancakes with Lemon Sauce

Ginger Pancakes

2 cups Bisquick (regular or reduced fat)

1 egg

1 1/3 cups milk

¼ cup light (or mild) molasses

1½ tsp. ground ginger

1 tsp. cinnamon

½ tsp. ground cloves

Beat ingredients with hand beater until smooth. Pour scant ¼ cup of batter onto hot griddle (greased if necessary). Fry until pancakes are dry around edges. Turn and fry other side.

Lemon Sauce

½ cup butter or margarine

1 cup sugar

¼ cup water

1 egg, well beaten

grated peel of one lemon

3 tbsp. fresh lemon juice (or the juice of one lemon)

Heat all ingredients to boiling over medium heat, stirring constantly.

Cream Cheese

Cut a 3-ounce package of cream cheese or Neufchatel into about 7 cubes.

To serve

Spread a cube of cream cheese on a pancake. Top with lemon sauce. Place another pancake on top of it. Top it with lemon sauce. This makes one serving. Serves 7.

French Pancakes

You can serve these delicate pancakes with any of the suggested fillings, or with your favorite syrup.

1 large egg
1 cup milk
2 tbsp. melted butter
1 cup flour
1½ tbsp. sugar
½ tsp. salt
2 level tsp. baking powder

In medium bowl, whip egg with fork, adding milk and butter. In separate bowl, add all dry ingredients and mix with wire whisk. Add dry ingredients to liquid, mixing with the whisk as you add, until batter is smooth.

Cook in slightly oiled pan or on a crepe pan, over medium heat. Turn when tops start to bubble and bottom is brown.

Fillings:

Spiced Apple

Beat together 1 cup lowfat cottage cheese, 1 cup cream cheese, 1/8 cup confectioner's sugar. Set aside. In a heavy saucepan, melt 1/3 cup margarine with 1/2 cup brown sugar, 1 tsp. cinnamon, and 1/4 tsp. nutmeg. Add 6 peeled, cored, and thinly sliced, tart apples. Sauté lightly. Fill pancakes with 3 to 4 tsp. cheese mixture and roll up. Bake at 300° for 10 minutes. Top with apple mixture.

Ham & Cheese

Dice ½ pound boiled or smoke ham. Sprinkle into crepes, then sprinkle with 1 ½ cups grated cheddar cheese. Roll up pancakes. In a bowl, blend a 10 oz can of cream of mushroom soup with ½ cup milk. Pour over pancakes. Sprinkle with 1 cup grated cheddar cheese. Broil until bubbly.

Cranberry Crumb Coffee Cake

1 cup all purpose flour
1 cup whole wheat flour
1 cup granulated sugar
2 tsp. cinnamon
½ cup margarine
1 large egg
1 cup buttermilk
1 tsp. almond flavoring
¾ tsp. baking soda
½ tsp. salt
1 12 ounce bag raw cranberries, washed*
pecans

Preheat oven to 375°. Mix the first four dry ingredients in a large bowl. Cut in margarine until large crumbs form. Set aside ¾ cup of this mixture for topping. Add next five ingredients and mix well. Fold in the cranberries. Grease and flour 9-inch cake pan. Pour mixture into pan and sprinkle with the saved crumb mixture and pecans. Bake 30 minutes.

* If fresh cranberries are not available, use unsulphured dried cranberries and reduce sugar to 2/3 cup.

For another wonderful topping, chop ¼ cup of cranberries and pecans in a food processor. Combine with reserved crumb mixture and top.

Peach Coffee Cake

Cake:
3 eggs
2 cups sugar
¾ cup vegetable oil
2 cups milk
½ tsp. salt
2 tsp. baking powder
4¼ cups flour
2 cups peaches, diced and drained

Filling:
1 cup cream cheese, softened
1/3 tsp. almond extract
2 tbsp. peach juice or peach nectar
¾ cup sugar

Topping:
1/3 cup cinnamon/sugar mixture

Preheat oven to 350°.

Cake: Combine the eggs, sugar, milk, oil, salt, baking powder, and flour in a large bowl. Beat 2 minutes then gently stir in the peaches. Spread into a 9" x 9" glass pan coated with cooking spray.

Filling: Combine filling ingredients and pour over cake mixture in pan. Then gently draw the blade of a knife through the filling and cake mixtures to create lines or webs.

Topping: Sprinkle over the top of filling.

Bake for 35 minutes or until center of cake is set and a toothpick inserted in center comes out clean.

Poached Apricots with Crème Fraiche

This is a delightful finish to a Sunday brunch. Crème fraiche is available in the dairy section of major grocery stores.

Apricots:
2 cups sugar
1¾ cups sweet white wine
1¼ cup water
1/8 tsp. salt
2 vanilla beans, split
12 fresh apricots, whole

Crème Fraiche:
½ cup crème fraiche
1 tbsp. sugar
½ tsp. vanilla
dash of salt

Garnish:
1 ½ cups blueberries
1 ½ cups raspberries

Apricots: Combine sugar, wine, water, and salt in a large saucepan. Scrape seeds from vanilla beans and add to mixture. Bring to a boil; add apricots. Reduce heat and simmer 2 minutes. Remove apricots. Bring wine mixture to boil again; cook until reduced to about 2 ¼ cups of liquid, about 20 minutes. Cool to room temperature. Pit apricots. Combine wine mixture and apricot halves; cover and chill at least 8 hours.

Crème Fraiche: Combine commercial crème, sugar, vanilla, and salt. Mix well.

To serve: Arrange 3 apricot halves on a serving plate with 3 tbsp. blueberries and 3 tbsp. raspberries. Drizzle with 2 tbsp. wine mixture. Top with a dollop of crème fraiche. Serves 8.

Feta, Walnut, & Pear Sandwiches

We've served these sophisticated sandwiches at many teas. They are fast becoming a favorite.

½ cup walnuts
10 oz. feta or blue cheese
1-2 tbsp. heavy cream or milk
½ ripe pear, cored
6 slices multi-grain bread
Flat-leaf parsley for garnish

Toast walnuts under the broiler and finely chop them. Place cheese into a small bowl and mash until soft. Add 1 tablespoon of cream or milk for creamy consistency (add second tablespoon if needed). Slice pear into 12 thin slices.

Spread bread with thin coating of butter. Divide cheese equally among 3 slices of bread, coating evenly. Place a heaping tablespoon of nuts over the cheese. Place 4 slices of pear on each sandwich and top with remaining slices of bread. Trim crusts from bread, cut each sandwich into 4 pieces and serve. Makes 3 sandwiches or 12 pieces.

Soups and Super Salads

Since its earliest days, Colorado has been a magnet for outdoor enthusiasts. The Rocky Mountains prove to be an irresistible draw for adventure seekers of all sorts. Rock climbing and mountain summiting are just a few of the outdoor sports that comprise Colorado's over 150 year history. Since 1912, the Colorado Mountain Club has been on the leading edge of outdoor education, recreation, and conservation. They help ensure a sustainable future for the Rocky Mountains.

(Photo: Bestor Robinson party on the knife ridge of Capitol Peak; courtesy of the Colorado Mountain Club)

Grilled Lemon Chicken Pasta Soup

2 tbsp. olive oil
½ cup onion, chopped
2 cloves garlic, minced
3 celery stalks, chopped
3 carrots, sliced
1 red bell pepper, diced
6 cups low-sodium chicken broth
2 cups water
2 cups farfalle pasta (bowtie)
2 or 3 chicken breasts, grilled and cut into small pieces
2 tbsp. fresh lemon juice
2 tsp. lemon zest
3 cups fresh spinach, chopped
    (do not use frozen)
salt and pepper
parmagiano chesse, grated

    Heat oil in a large heavy pot over medium heat. Add onion and garlic, stir for 1 minute. Add celery, carrot, and bell pepper and sauté until tender, about 7 minutes. Add the broth and water and bring to boil. Reduce heat and simmer about 20 minutes on low heat. Add pasta and cook until it is tender, about 10 minutes, stirring occasionally. Add chicken, lemon juice, lemon zest, and spinach and cook only until spinach is wilted, but still bright green, about 3 minutes. Serve this soup with more broth if desired. Season with salt and pepper to taste. Serve with grated parmagiano.

Carrot and Orange Soup

4 tbsp. sweet butter
2 cups finely chopped yellow onion
12 large carrots, (1½ - 2 lbs.) peeled and chopped
4 cups chicken stock
1 cup fresh orange juice
salt and freshly ground black pepper to taste
grated fresh orange zest to taste

Melt the butter in a pot. Add the onions. Cover and cook over low heat until tender and lightly colored, about 25 minutes. Add the carrots and stock and bring to a boil. Reduce heat, cover, and simmer until carrots are very tender, about 30 minutes. Pour the soup through a strainer and transfer the solids to a blender or food processor. Add one cup of the cooking stock and process until smooth. Return the puree to the pot and add the orange juice and additional stock, 2 – 3 cups, until soup is of desired consistency. Season to taste with salt and pepper. Add orange zest. Simmer until heated through. Serve immediately. Serves 4 – 6.

Golden Lager Cheese Soup

1/4 cup butter or margarine
1/4 cup all-purpose flour
2 cans (12 fl. oz. each) evaporated milk
1 cup Coors Golden Lager beer
2 tsp. Worcestershire sauce

1/2 tsp. dry mustard (optional)
1/4 tbsp. cayenne pepper
2 cups sharp cheddar cheese, shredded
Toppings: crumbled cooked bacon, sliced
green onions, croutons

Melt butter in large saucepan. Add flour; cook, stirring constantly, until bubbly. Add evaporated milk; bring to a boil, stirring constantly. Reduce heat; stir in beer, Worcestershire sauce, mustard and cayenne pepper. Simmer for 10 minutes. Remove from heat. Stir in cheese until melted. Season with salt. Serve in heavy bowls with desired toppings.

Squash and Pear Soup

1 pound butternut squash
1 large yam
1½ cups vegetable broth
1½ cups water
1 tsp. ground cinnamon
¾ tsp. salt
2 tbsp. butter
1 medium onion, sliced
2 medium canned Bartlett pears
1/3 cup dry white wine
¼ cup half and half
white pepper to taste

Peel, seed, and dice squash. Peel and dice yam. Put both in pot with vegetable broth and water, cinnamon, and salt. Simmer until tender, about 35 minutes.

Melt butter and gently cook onions, stirring occasionally until they begin to caramelize. Thinly slice pears and add them to the onions. Continue cooking for about 5 minutes, stirring often. Add the wine and cover. Simmer for 10 minutes. Add pear mixture to soup and puree all in blender in batches. Add the half and half and some white pepper and a pinch of salt, if needed. Heat soup to simmer but do not boil. May garnish with chopped chives or sprigs of cilantro. Serves 6.

Chili Dumpling Stew

1 can (1lb 4 oz) red kidney beans
2½ cups raw potatoes, cubed
1 tbsp. salt
½ tsp. pepper
4 cup water
½ cup onion, chopped
1 pound ground beef
2 tsp. chili powder
1 can (10 ½ oz) condensed tomato soup

In 5 quart saucepan combine undrained kidney beans with potatoes, 2 tsp. salt, pepper, and water; bring to a boil. While mixture boils, heat shortening in skillet. Sauté onion until tender; add beef, chili powder and 1 tsp. salt; cook until meat is well browned. Add meat mixture and tomato soup; stir well; simmer 1 hour. Return to boil and add dumplings.

Egg Dumplings
1 ½ cups flour
4 tsp. baking powder
½ tsp. salt
1 beaten egg
¼ cup milk
½ tsp. nutmeg
1 tbsp. butter

Stir together first 3 ingredients. In a separate bowl, mix the next 4 ingredients and stir into flour. Drop by spoonfuls onto boiling stew. Cover tightly, steam (without lifting lid) until done, 12 to 15 minutes.

Roasted Mushroom Soup

Mushroom stock:

4 cups dried wild mushrooms, several varieties

10½ cups cold water

8 ounces fresh Portobello mushrooms, sliced

4 ounces fresh shitake mushrooms (no stems), chopped

8 ounces fresh button mushrooms, chopped

kosher salt, divided use: 2 tsp. and ½ tsp.

canola oil, divided use: 3 tbsp. and 2 tbsp.

1 large yellow onion, chopped

1 medium carrot, chopped

2 stalks celery, chopped

1 tsp. garlic powder

1 tsp. onion powder

1 tsp. white pepper

2 tsp. dried basil

½ tsp. dried thyme

1 bay leaf

1¾ cup heavy cream

Roux:

½ cup unsalted butter

½ cup all-purpose flour

Several drops truffle oil (optional)

Put dried mushrooms in a large pot and cover with the cold water. Bring to a boil and lower heat. Cover and simmer 45 minutes. Strain, reserving stock and discarding mushrooms. Meanwhile, combine fresh mushrooms in a bowl and toss well in 3 tablespoons oil and 2 teaspoons salt. Spread mushrooms on a large sheet pan and roast in a preheated 450 degree oven for about 20 minutes. Remove from oven. In a large stockpot over medium-high heat, sauté the onion, carrot and celery with 2 tablespoons oil and ½ teaspoon salt until tender. Add seasonings, except bay leaf, and sauté 2 minutes more, stirring often. Add the roasted mushrooms and stir. Add the mushroom stock, bay leaf, and heavy cream. Bring to a simmer, cover and gently simmer for 1 hour and 15 minutes. During the last 15 minutes of simmering the soup, make a roux in a small pan. Melt the butter over medium heat; stir in flour. Stir constantly for about 5 minutes so that you have a smooth paste. When the soup is finished, remove the bay leaf. Whisk in roux and simmer for 10 minutes more. Using a hand blender, puree soup at high speed until smooth. Allow soup to rest overnight in refrigerator before serving. To serve, heat and garnish each individual serving with a few drops of truffle oil (optional).

Spicy Chicken Tortilla Soup

Broth

6 chicken breasts with bone for flavor
2 whole carrots - chunked
1 onion - chunked
salt and peppercorns to taste
8 cups water

Cook chicken until tender. Cook the day before you want to make the soup. Cool overnight and skim fat off before starting the soup. Cut chicken off bone; cube or shred. Strain broth; be sure you have at least 8 cups of broth. Add canned chicken broth if your soup is too thick.

1 cup chopped onion	2 12 oz. cans whole kernel corn, undrained
2 cloves garlic, minced	3 tsp. ground cumin
3 tbsp. vegetable oil	1 tsp. black pepper
6 medium zucchini, diced	2 tsp. garlic powder
1 can Rotel tomatoes with green chilies - medium or hot, your choice	1 tsp. salt
	tortilla chips
1 15 oz. can stewed tomatoes, undrained	1 cup shredded Monterey Jack Cheese
1 15 oz. can tomato sauce	

Make chicken broth the day before. Sauté onions and garlic in oil. Add zucchini. Sauté until just beginning to soften. Have broth hot and add the sautéed vegetables, all can ingredients, spices, and chicken. Do not add tortilla chips and cheese. Cover and simmer for 45 minutes. Spoon into bowls and add chips and cheese.

Note: Makes a huge amount; freezes well.

Tortilla Soup

Soup:
6 quarts chicken broth
*2 pasillas or Serrano chiles, 2 Ancho chiles, washed, seeded and sautéed
4 tomatoes, peeled
1 onion, sliced
4 cloves garlic, diced
2/3 cup olive oil
2 sprigs cilantro
*2 Anaheim chiles, peeled, seeded, chopped and sautéed in oil
salt

In a blender combine chiles, tomatoes, onion, and garlic. Process 2 minutes. Strain. Heat oil in a large stockpot. Pour mixture into pot and cook over medium high heat until mixture thickens and fat rises to surface. Add cilantro, broth and Anaheim chiles. Season with salt to taste. Simmer 25 minutes.

Garnish:
2 cups vegetable oil
24 corn tortillas, sliced in thin strips and slightly stale
2 avocados, peeled and sliced
*2 cups panela or feta cheese, crumbled
*1 cup crema or 1 cup sour cream mixed with ¼ cup half-n-half
sliced jalapenos, serranos, or Anaheim chiles, to taste

Heat oil in frying pan and quickly fry the tortilla strips until crisp. Dry on folded paper towels. Sprinkle with salt.

To serve: ladle soup into bowls, sprinkle with tortilla strips. Serve with remaining garnish items.

*Most major grocery stores carry these items now; for panela and crema, look in the dairy case. Crema comes in a jar. Grocery stores located along Federal and Sheridan Blvds. in Denver stock all of these items.

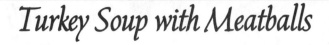
Turkey Soup with Meatballs

1 meaty turkey frame
additional chopped cooked turkey meat
8 cups water
1 large onion, quartered
½ tsp. garlic
1/8 tsp. salt
1 14 ounce can diced tomatoes
1 tbsp. chicken bouillon granules
1 tsp. oregano

1 tsp. thyme
¼ tsp. pepper
1 cup celery, diced
1 cup carrot, diced
1 small onion, chopped
½ cup mushrooms, diced
1½ cups dried egg noodles
Meatballs (recipe below)

Cut turkey frame in half with large knife or kitchen shears. Place into large stockpot; cover with water. Add quartered onion, garlic, and salt. Bring to boil; reduce heat and simmer covered for 1½ hours. Remove bones and cut meat from bones. Chop meat and add enough additional meat to equal 2 cups. Set aside. Discard bones. Skim fat from broth and strain. Return broth to pot. Stir in tomatoes, bouillon, herbs, pepper, vegetables, and meatballs. Return to boiling; reduce heat and cover. Simmer 15 minutes. Add noodles and simmer additional 10 minutes or until vegetables are crisp-tender. Stir in turkey and heat through.

Meatballs:
1 egg
3 tbsp. grated Parmesan cheese
3 whole squares of saltine crackers or 12 single crackers
1 tbsp. minced parsley
1 clove minced garlic
½ lb. ground pork or spicy sausage
1 tsp. salt
dash of pepper

Mix all the ingredients together and form into small meatballs.

Colorado Mountain Club

710 10th Street, Suite 200
Golden, CO 80401
303.279.3080 or
800.633.4417
www.cmc.org

Founded in 1912, the Colorado Mountain Club is the largest non-profit outdoor education, recreation, and conservation organization of its kind in the Rocky Mountains. Membership in the Colorado Mountain Club provides:

Outdoor Education: Schools, seminars, and courses that teach outdoor skills through hands-on activities. Wilderness trekking, rock climbing, high altitude mountaineering, backpacking, and much more.

Spicy Chili

3 lbs. ground chuck
    (or 85% lean ground beef)
1 onion, diced
1 green pepper, diced
2 cans diced tomatoes
2 cans whole tomatoes
2 cans dark red kidney beans
1 tsp. salt
1 tbsp. pepper
1½ tbsp. chili powder
1 tbsp. cayenne pepper

Toppings: green onions, jalapenos, sour cream, extra sharp cheddar cheese, and a squeeze of lime

Brown the hamburger and drain grease into another pan. Sauté 1 whole diced onion and 1 whole diced green pepper in the meat drippings. Once browned, add the onion/green pepper to the browned meat. Add the diced tomatoes, whole tomatoes, and dark red kidney beans. Add salt, pepper, chili powder, and cayenne pepper to taste. Simmer for about 1 hour. Stir occasionally to prevent burning on the bottom. Add toppings as desired. Can serve with garlic bread.

Ham Chowder

This makes an easy supper using any leftover ham.

1 cup cooked ham, chopped
1 medium onion, chopped
1½ tbsp. butter
1 cup cold water
1 cup potato, peeled and diced
2 tbsp. flour

½ tsp. salt
½ tsp. pepper
2 cups warm milk
1 can cream style corn

Brown ham and onion in butter. Add potatoes and cold water. Cover and cook until tender. Blend flour, salt, and pepper with ½ cup milk. Add to the meat and potatoes. Add remaining milk and corn. Simmer 10 minutes until slightly thick.

"Hot" Tomato Soup

1 ½ tbsp. oil
½ diced onion
2 cloves garlic
2 fresh jalapenos, diced
1 28 oz. can whole tomatoes, drained
3 cups chicken broth
1 tsp. salt
¼ cup grated cheddar cheese

Cook onion and garlic in hot oil until soft. Add jalapenos and tomatoes and cook about 5 minutes until mixture is slightly thickened. Stir in chicken broth and salt and heat through. Garnish with cheese.

Colorado Mountain Club

Continued
Conservation:
Making your voice heard on important issues, we work with agencies and partners to develop responsible land management programs, spearhead vital legislation, and create a sustainable future for the Rocky Mountains.

Outdoor Recreation:
Over 3100 trips and outings led annually. Hike, ski, climb, backpack, snowshoe, bicycle, ice skate, travel the world, build friendships.

The American Mountaineering Center:
A world-class facility featuring the largest mountaineering library in the western hemisphere, a 300-seat auditorium, a technical climbing wall, and a planned mountaineering museum.

GREAT
Golden Resource for Education, Arts, and Theater

P.O. Box 702
Golden, CO 80402
303.279.0721

The Golden Resource for Education, Arts, and Theater (GREAT) is a non-profit organization established in 2001 dedicated to enhancing, promoting, and enriching the Golden community's cultural diversity in relation to the cinematic and performing arts. GREAT serves as a resource to facilitate the development of a variety of film-related experiences for families of, and visitors to, Golden, Jefferson County, and the mountain communities west of Denver.

Best-Ever Bean Soup

2 cups dried assorted beans*
2 quarts water
ham bone or ham hocks
1 large onion, chopped
1 clove garlic, minced
1 20 oz. can of diced or
    stewed tomatoes

1 tsp. chili powder
2 tsp. cumin
salt and pepper to taste
1 lemon, juiced

Wash beans thoroughly and place in a large kettle. Cover with water. Add one tablespoon of salt and soak overnight. Drain and add two quarts of water and ham or ham hocks. Simmer slowly for 1½ - 3 hours. Add onion, garlic, tomatoes, chili powder, cumin, salt, and pepper. Simmer another half hour or more. Remove ham bone or ham hocks. Serve with cornbread.

* black beans, navy beans, split peas, black-eyed peas, lima beans and lentils are good choices

Split Pea Soup

This takes a bit of time to prepare, but it's worth it! Feel free to add more celery and/or carrots.

2 cups (1 package) dried split peas
2 quarts water
2 celery stalks, chopped
2 carrots, chopped

1 small onion, chopped
¼ tsp. thyme
1 bay leaf
salt to taste
pinch of garlic powder

Put all ingredients in a large pot and boil hard for 20 minutes. Reduce heat and simmer for about an hour or until the peas are done. If you like a chunky soup, mix with a mixer. If you prefer a smoother consistency, use a blender.

Chilled Blueberry Soup

2 pt. blueberries
2 cups plain yogurt
½ cup sugar
1 cup water
1/4 tsp. cinnamon
½ cup orange juice

Place blueberries, sugar, water, and cinnamon in a saucepan over medium heat about 15 minutes until berries are tender, stirring often. Remove from heat and stir in yogurt and orange juice. Pour half of mixture into blender and puree. Pour into covered container and repeat with remaining mixture. Chill in refrigerator until cold.

GREAT
Golden Resource for Education, Arts, and Theater

Continued

GREAT has sponsored several events, including an evening of Colorado-based silent film clips accompanied by a historical lecture, two summer movies in the park, a classic film series, and the first Golden Film Festival, GREAT's signature event, showcasing Oscar-nominated feature length and short documentaries, short live action films, animated shorts, and Colorado-produced student films. Working with city officials, business owners, civic organizations, local clubs, individuals, and volunteers, the group seeks to generate support for cultural entities who desire to enter the Golden market.

Beef Stew

2 lbs. round steak, cubed
flour
2 tbsp. oil
1 lb. large onions, thickly sliced
2 – 3 cloves garlic
1 large can beef broth
1 tbsp. red wine vinegar

1 bay leaf
¼ cup parsley
1 tsp. thyme
1½ tbsp. dark brown sugar
12 oz. beer
1 tbsp. red wine vinegar

Dredge steak in flour and brown in hot oil with onions and garlic. Remove meat and onions. Add broth, 1 tbsp. vinegar, bay leaf, parsley, thyme, and brown sugar. Deglaze pan. Return beef and onions. Cover and refrigerate overnight.

Next day, add beer and bake, covered, at 350° for 3½ - 4 hours. Remove from oven. Stir in remaining 1 tbsp. vinegar. Bring to a boil and stir on top of stove.

Serve over noodles.

Peanut Soup

2 tbsp. butter
1 tbsp. vegetable oil
1 small onion, chopped
2 medium celery stalks, chopped
2 tbsp. flour
4 cups chicken stock or broth
1 cup creamy peanut butter

¼ cup heavy cream or half and half
1½ tsp. salt
1 tsp. ground red pepper
1 tsp. hot red pepper sauce
2 tsp. fresh lemon juice
3 tbsp. dry roasted peanuts
¼ cup chopped scallion greens

Melt butter and oil in soup pot. Add onion and celery and cook until tender, but not browned. Stir in flour. Reduce heat to low and cook, stirring, for about 5 minutes. Stir in chicken stock or broth. Simmer, stirring often, about 5 minutes or until soup starts to thicken. Stir in peanut butter, cream, salt, red pepper and pepper sauce. Heat through, but do not boil. Add lemon juice and garnish with peanuts and scallions.

Spanish Chicken Soup

2 whole boneless and skinless chicken breasts
1 qt. chicken broth
pinch oregano
1 cup cooked rice
1 cup garbanzo beans, cooked
    (drain well if using canned)

1 ripe avocado, pitted and peeled
1 chipotle chili, minced
4 – 6 oz. Monterey Jack or Havarti cheese
4 sprigs cilantro

Put chicken in the pot with the broth. Bring to a boil, then reduce heat to a simmer and poach for 12 minutes. Remove from the pot and cut into thin strips (1 1/2 inches long). Return the chicken to the broth and add oregano, rice, garbanzo beans, avocado, and chipotle.

Divide the cheese into four soup bowls. Heat soup to boiling and ladle over cheese. Garnish with cilantro.

This dish may be made a day ahead, but do not add the avocado until you reheat the soup to serve.

Chili Verde (Green Chili)

1½ pounds pork shoulder, cubed
2 tbsp. vegetable oil
4 cups canned diced tomatoes
½ cup chicken broth
½ small onion, diced
1 clove garlic, minced

¼ tsp. sugar
7 ounces green chilies, chopped
1 tsp. cumin
2 tbsp. lemon juice
3 tbsp. cilantro
salt to taste

In a medium stockpot, brown the pork in oil. Add remaining ingredients and simmer, covered, for 2 hours or until flavors blend.

Butternut Squash Soup with Apple Confit

3 cups vegetable stock
1 tbsp. olive oil
1 medium yellow onion, thinly sliced
salt to taste
white pepper to taste
4 lbs. butternut squash, peeled, seeded,
   and cut into large cubes, about 6 cups

3 tbsp. Calvados
1 tbsp. unsalted butter
2 McIntosh or other flavorful, not too
   tart, apples, peeled, cored, and sliced,
   about 2 ½ cups
½ cup apple juice
½ cup crème fraiche

Heat olive oil in a soup pot and add the onion, ½ teaspoon salt, and a pinch of pepper. Sauté over medium heat until the onions slightly caramelize, about 15 minutes, adding a little stock and using a wooden spoon to scrape them as they stick to the pan. Add 2 tablespoons of the Calvados and cook for 1 or 2 minutes, until pan is almost dry.

Add squash and 1 teaspoon of salt to the onions. Add just enough stock to barely cover the squash (about 2 cups); the squash breaks down quickly and releases its own liquid as it cooks. Cover the pot and cook over medium heat for 20 - 30 minutes, until the squash is very soft. Puree the soup in a blender or food processor, and thin it with stock to reach the desired consistency. Return the pureed soup to the pot, cover, and cook over low heat for 30 minutes.

While the soup is cooking, make the apple confit. Melt butter in a medium sized sauté pan and add the apples; sauté over medium high heat, stirring to coat them with the butter. When they're heated through, add the remaining Calvados and cook for 1 or 2 minutes, until the pan is almost dry. Add the apple juice, cover the pan, and cook over medium heat for 15 - 20 minutes, or until soft. Cook, uncovered, for 8 - 10 minutes to reduce the liquid. Mash the apples, making sure the confit retains some texture.

Stir half the confit into the soup, saving the rest to stir into each serving. Season the soup with salt and pepper to taste. Add a spoonful of apple confit and a swirl of crème fraiche to each serving. Makes 8 - 9 cups.

Real Hillbilly Chili

This chili recipe for a crowd comes from North Carolina. In the absence of homemade Moonshine, feel free to substitute Jack Daniels Black Label whiskey. It makes about 3 gallons of chili.

1 large onion, chopped*
1-2 green bell peppers, chopped
12-16oz canned sliced mushrooms**
6-8 15oz cans light red kidney beans
3 large cans whole stewed tomatoes
3 cans tomato sauce ***
4 ½ - 6 lbs. meat per gallon of chili
(burger, steak, roast, venison, or
    whatever you have cut it into
    bite-size pieces and trim fat)

3 - 4 heaping tbsp. black pepper
5 heaping tbsp. chili powder (to taste)
1 ½ tbsp. salt
large dash A-1 sauce or Worcestershire sauce
½ - 1 cup pickle juice (brine)
3 - 4 1/2 jiggers Moonshine
    or Jack Daniels Black Label
1 oz Parmesan cheese****
garlic salt and/or seasoning salt, to taste
3 bay leaves

In a large pot (5 gal. gumbo pot is great) melt 1 tbsp. shortening over high heat. Cook onions till clear. Add meat. Cook till brown. While meat cooks, season well with salt, black pepper, and garlic salt. As you stir the meat, gradually add seasonings till well seasoned. Do this in stages. The meat will taste different before seasoning and after. Drain, leaving a little fat for flavor. Add mushrooms and bell pepper. Reduce heat to medium. Add beans, tomatoes, tomato sauce and stir well. Add salt, black pepper, chili powder, pickle juice, liquor, and maybe some more garlic salt, parmesan cheese, and bay leaf. Stir well. Taste and adjust seasoning as necessary. Cover pot and simmer on low heat for about an hour, stirring well regularly to prevent burning. Check taste periodically and add anything else if you think it needs a little more pizzazz. It's best to cook this the night before you need it and let it stand overnight, covered.

Notes:

* Chop onion and pepper into large chunks, large enough to see and taste.

** If you prefer to use fresh mushrooms, wash, slice, and sauté in butter before adding to chili.

*** Tomato paste will do if you like thick chili - 3 or 4 large cans.

**** If you should put too much A-1, Worcestershire, or whatever - more Parmesan will mellow it out.

Potato & Turnip Soup

1 lb. Yukon Gold potatoes, peeled and diced
2 turnips, peeled and diced
1 qt. good stock, beef or chicken (to your taste)
6 oz. assorted mushrooms (shitake, crimini, morel or porcini) diced.*
2 oz. fresh parmesan or asiago cheese, shaved
2 tbsp. olive oil
2 tbsp. butter
½ cup light cream

Boil potatoes and turnips until mashable. Mash with 1 tablespoon butter and cream until smooth. Add salt and pepper to taste. Sauté mushrooms in olive oil until well-browned. Add stock and simmer until a nice dark sauce develops. Use a buerre (a previously cooked flour and butter mix), one teaspoon at a time to thicken the mushroom sauce to your taste.

In an open soup bowl place the potato-turnip mix. Use a spoon to form a bowl in the center to hold the mushroom soup. Ladle the mushroom soup into the formed potato bowl. Sprinkle with grated cheese just before serving.

The turnips add a subtle flavor to the mix that surprises the senses.

*Should you be able to afford truffles, the results will be extraordinary.

Grandmother's Veggie Beef Soup

Beef, with bone (This can be ox tails, left-over prime rib or steak, etc. Less beef is actually better than more, as too much meat will make the soup stringy. Stay away from stew beef or a roast, for instance.)

3 - 4 large potatoes
5 - 7 large carrots
3 - 5 medium onions
1 rutabaga
1 turnip
3 - 4 stalks celery (optional)
2 bay leaves
salt and pepper to taste

Cook the beef and bones slowly in a pot of water either several hours or all day or night in a large crock pot. Cool and separate the meat from the bones, putting the meat back in the pot and saving the bones for doggie treats. Spoon off the excess fat on the top of the broth, or use a fat-separator measuring cup.

Bring back to a low boil and add the veggies, cut into rather large pieces (two - three pieces per soup spoonful). Add the bay leaves, salt and pepper. Make sure the broth is covering the veggies. If not, add more water. Cook slowly for several hours or in a crock pot all day.

Remove the bay leaves and check the seasoning before serving. Serve with French bread or Bisquick biscuits and salad, accompanied by red wine and a cozy fire.

Spicy Red Bean Soup

Place in cheesecloth bag:

1 tsp. cayenne pepper

1 tsp. freshly ground pepper

2 bay leaves, crumbled

1 tsp. ground cumin

Soup:

1 lb. dry red beans, washed

3 quarts water

1¼ lbs. lean smoked ham hock

1 tbsp. salt

1½ cups chopped celery, cut into ½" pieces

1½ cups chopped onion

2 cloves minced garlic

½ tsp. Tabasco sauce

3 tbsp. minced fresh parsley

Except for Tabasco sauce and minced fresh parsley, simmer ingredients covered for 3 - 4 hours, stirring occasionally. Just before serving, remove spice ball. Stir in Tabasco and parsley. Pass extra Tabasco sauce.

Flavor improves if soup is made one day ahead. Try serving this soup over hot rice or cornbread muffins on the side for a hearty southern-style meal.

Pebble Salad

2 1/3 cups water
1 pkg. (6 oz.) long grain and wild rice
1 can (12 oz.) white shoe peg corn, drained or 1 can (12 oz.) whole kernel corn, drained
1 small cucumber, seeded and chopped
2 medium carrots, coarsely chopped
2 green onions w/tops, thinly sliced
1/3 cup fresh parsley, chopped
1/3 cup olive oil or vegetable oil
¼ cup lemon juice
2 cloves garlic, minced
½ tsp. dill weed
¼ tsp. dry mustard
¼ tsp. pepper
½ cup dry roasted sunflower seeds
Romaine lettuce
1/3 cup slivered almonds

Bring water and contents of rice and seasoning packets to boil in medium saucepan. Cover tightly and simmer until all liquid is absorbed, about 25 minutes. Transfer to large bowl. Cool to room temperature. Stir corn, cucumber, carrots, onions and parsley into rice. Combine lemon juice, oil, garlic, dill, mustard and pepper in small bowl. Mix well. Stir into rice mixture. Refrigerate, covered, several hours or overnight. Stir in sunflower seeds. Serve on a lettuce-lined plate. Sprinkle with almonds.

Honey Marinated Melon

½ cup honey
¼ cup water
¼ cup lime juice
1 cup watermelon balls or cubes
1 cup cantaloupe balls or cubes
1 cup honeydew balls or cubes

In a small saucepan, combine honey and water. Bring to a boil; reduce heat and simmer 5 minutes. Stir in lime juice. Cool completely.

In a large bowl, combine watermelon, cantaloupe, and honeydew. Pour cooled marinade over fruit. Cover. Refrigerate 1 – 2 hours. Makes eight ½ cup servings.

Frog Eye Salad

1 box R&F Ancine De-Pepe noodles
Sauce:
    ½ tsp. salt
    1 cup sugar
    2 tbsp. flour
    1 ¾ cup pineapple juice
    3 egg yolks, beaten until stiff
2 cans mandarin oranges
1 can pineapple tidbits
½ bag colored mini-marshmallows, optional
8 oz. Cool Whip

Cook noodles for 10 – 15 minutes. Drain and cool. Combine rest of sauce ingredients and cook in saucepan until thick. Pour sauce over noodles. Cover tightly and refrigerate overnight. Add fruit, marshmallows, and Cool Whip. Mix well and refrigerate.

Four Fruit Salad

1 20 oz. can pineapple chunks
½ cup sugar
2 tbsp. cornstarch
1/3 cup orange juice
1 tbsp. lemon juice
1 11 oz. can mandarin oranges, drained
4 apples, unpeeled and chopped
3 bananas, sliced

Drain pineapple, reserving ¾ cup juice. In a saucepan, combine sugar and cornstarch. Add the pineapple juice and orange and lemon juices. Cook and stir over medium heat until thickened and bubbly. Remove from heat. Set aside. Combine pineapple chunks, oranges, apples, and bananas. Pour the warm sauce over the fruit, stirring gently to coat. Cover and refrigerate. Serves 12 – 16.

Orange Buttermilk Salad

This is a family favorite for holiday meals.

1 can (8 oz.) crushed pineapple
6-ounce package orange Jell-O
2 cups buttermilk
8 ounces whipped topping
¼ cup pecans, chopped

Bring crushed pineapple with juice to a boil. Remove from heat and add Jell-O. Stir until Jell-O is dissolved. Cool to room temperature. Stir in buttermilk, then fold in whipped topping and pecans. Chill 4 hours or overnight. Serves 6 – 8.

Frozen Fruit Salad

1 8 oz. package cream cheese
¾ cup sugar
1 large can pineapple chunks, well drained
1 10 oz. package frozen sliced strawberries, thawed
½ cup chopped nuts
2 bananas, sliced
1 9oz. container of Cool Whip, thawed

Whip cream cheese and sugar together; set aside. In separate bowl, combine remaining ingredients. Combine both mixtures and pour into a waxed paper-lined loaf pan. Freeze. Note: This salad will keep in the freezer for 4 weeks.

Mixed Vegetable Salad

1 can green beans
1 can peas
1 can whole corn
1 onion (diced)
1 green pepper (diced)
1 small red pepper or small jar pimentos
½ tsp. salt
¼ tsp. pepper
¾ cup sugar
¼ cup cooking oil
¾ cup vinegar, cider or white
1 tbsp. water

Drain vegetables well; mix together in large bowl. In saucepan, combine last six ingredients and heat to dissolve sugar, but do not boil. Cool mixture to room temperature. Pour dressing over vegetables; stir once and allow time to marinate. Refrigerate. Serves 10.

Caesar Salad Dressing

1 cup olive oil
1 tbsp. lemon juice
1 tbsp. white vinegar
1 tbsp. red wine vinegar
1 tbsp. Worcestershire sauce
2 whole raw eggs
1 tsp. salt
1/3 cup grated parmesan cheese
6 - 8 cloves fresh garlic

Place all ingredients but garlic in blender or food processor. Add garlic cloves one at a time. Taste after four cloves to see if it's garlic-y enough.

Great on a salad, chilled green beans, Chinese cabbage or to dip celery or carrot sticks in for a quick meal.

Marinated Tomatoes

I always use the herbs not in parentheses and sometimes use some or all of the others, depending on my preference. Fresh herbs are great if available, but dried will do.

Marinade:
olive oil
red wine vinegar or tarragon vinegar
sugar or artificial sweetener
salt
pepper
(basil)
dill weed
marjoram
thyme
(parsley)
(garlic)
(oregano)
Fresh tomatoes, 1 per person
Red onion

Parboil tomatoes for about 15 seconds, and then slip the skins off. Slice them fairly thick. Plan on one medium tomato per person. Peel and thinly slice onion. Separate into rings or chop.

Place a layer of tomatoes and then a layer of onions in a large, shallow bowl. Season with the above listed herbs and spices, about a generous pinch of each, and about 1 – 2 teaspoons of sugar or the equivalent artificial sweetening powder. Add another layer of tomatoes topped by onions, more herbs, and spices until you have prepared the quantity you want.

Top with oil and vinegar. I use equal quantities of oil and red wine vinegar. Toss well but carefully and marinate at least a few hours before serving.

Broccoli Salad

Dressing:
1 tsp. salt
1 tsp. dry mustard
1/3 cup sugar
¼ cup vinegar
1 cup salad oil

To make the dressing, mix first four dressing ingredients together. Chill overnight in refrigerator or 45 minutes in freezer. With electric mixer or hand beater, slowly beat in, salad oil. Beat until mixture is as thick as honey.

2 quarts broccoli florets, broken into small pieces
1 cup raisins, slightly softened in hot water or microwave
6 or 7 pieces of crisp bacon, broken into small pieces
1 cup cashews

Coat broccoli, raisins and bacon with dressing and refrigerate covered, stirring in cashews about 30 minutes before serving. Add dressing according to your taste.

Iowa Pea Salad

3 strips bacon, cooked and crumbled
2 cups cooked baby peas
1 cup mayonnaise
1 cup cooked macaroni
½ cup chopped green onion
½ cup grated cheddar cheese

Blend together all ingredients except for cheese. Refrigerate. Just before serving sprinkle with cheese.

Lariat Trail Salad

1 bunch of broccoli including stems, chopped
½ cup raisins
¼ cup chopped onion
8 slices bacon, fried and crumbled
½ cup grated cheddar cheese
¾ cup mayonnaise
¼ cup sugar
2 tbsp. white vinegar

Mix all ingredients together. Refrigerate overnight. Serves 12.

Bean Salad

½ cup sugar
½ cup vegetable oil
¾ cup vinegar
1 tsp. salt
1 16 oz. can green beans
1 16 oz. can wax beans
1 24 oz. can kidney beans
1 16 oz. can garbanzo beans
1 medium onion, chopped

Combine all ingredients, chill and serve. Makes 6 servings.

Blackened Chicken Salad with Raspberry Vinaigrette

12 ounces boneless, skinless chicken breasts
1 tbsp. olive oil
2 cloves garlic, crushed
½ tsp. blackened seasoning
¼ cup olive oil
¼ cup seedless red raspberry jam
¼ cup balsamic vinegar
6 cups mixed leaf lettuces
2 cups fresh or frozen raspberries (thawed and drained)
¼ cup sliced almonds or pine nuts, toasted

In a large skillet over high heat, sauté the garlic in 1 tbsp. olive oil just until it sweats. Coat chicken slices with blackened seasoning. Add to garlic. Stir to coat. Let chicken cook through and brown, about 12 minutes, stirring occasionally. Remove from heat. This step can be done on a grill; however, slice chicken after grilling.

Dressing:

In a small saucepan over medium heat, gently warm jam until it thins; whisk in balsamic vinegar. Remove from heat and whisk in olive oil

In a large bowl, arrange lettuce leaves and mound chicken in the center of lettuce. Sprinkle almonds and raspberries over the top. Serve with vinaigrette. Makes a wonderful main dish salad.

Pear, Walnut, & Blue Cheese Salad

The Golden Pioneer Museum hosts an annual salad luncheon. This salad, and various modifications on it, is always a popular dish. The combination of sweet and crisp pears with rich, creamy blue cheese is extraordinary.

Vinaigrette:
½ cup whole berry cranberry sauce
¼ cup orange juice
1 tbsp. extra virgin cold pressed olive oil
2 tbsp. Modena balsamic vinegar
1 tsp. sugar
1 tsp. fresh ginger, peeled and minced
¼ tsp. salt

Whisk together all ingredients; set aside.

Salad:
1 head Romaine lettuce
2 cups Bosc or D'Anjou pears, peeled and sliced
2 tbsp. orange juice
1 cup red or Maui onion, sliced very thin and separated
1/3 cup crumbled blue cheese
2 tbsp. walnuts (pecans are good too), toasted and chopped

Wash and pat dry the Romaine leaves. Tear each leaf in half. Layer in a serving bowl. Toss pears with orange juice. Arrange pears in bowl. Sprinkle remaining ingredients over lettuce and pears. Serve a salad portion topped with 2½ tbsp. vinaigrette. Serves 6

Super Salad

Use *all* or just some of the suggested salad ingredients. Whatever you choose will make a fabulous salad.

Salad Ingredients:

1 head iceberg lettuce,
    torn into bite-sized pieces
1 head other fancy lettuce
    (red-leaf, Romaine, Bibb), washed,
    dried, torn
2 – 3 tomatoes, chopped
1 cucumber, peeled and sliced thin
2 -3 scallions, sliced thin,
    or 1/2 red onion, sliced thin in rings
1 red, yellow, or green pepper

salad croutons
cheese (cheddar, provolone, or blue)
1 – 2 carrots, thinly sliced
broccoli, cut into small pieces
cauliflower, cut into small pieces
1 can of marinated artichokes, diced
1 can of hearts of palm, diced
1 can black olives, whole or cut
1 can of tiny marinated asparagus
1 small can of mandarin oranges

Mustard-Vinaigrette Salad Dressing:

4 oz. light olive oil
3 tbsp. almond or walnut oil
4 – 5 tbsp. balsamic vinegar
2 tbsp. Dijon-type mustard
salt to taste
fresh ground pepper to taste

Shake the above dressing ingredients vigorously together. Refrigerate if not using for several hours. This makes more than you will need for this amount of salad. The dressing keeps very well refrigerated and is delicious with other things such as a salad of watercress, Belgian endive, and enoki mushrooms. Also great as a dip for raw vegetables.

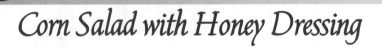

Corn Salad with Honey Dressing

1 bag (16 ounces) frozen corn
1 red bell pepper, diced
1 tbsp. fresh chives, chopped
3 tbsp. cider vinegar
1 tbsp. honey
½ tsp. celery seed
1/8 tsp. salt

Place the corn in a colander and rinse with hot water to thaw. Place in a large bowl and add the pepper and chives. Toss to combine. In a small saucepan, combine the vinegar, honey, celery seed, and salt. Cook over medium heat for 1 to 2 minutes or until honey thins. Pour over corn mixture and toss to coat. Serve at room temperature or chilled.

Serves 4.

Cranberry Slaw

1 cup spiced rice wine
½ cup canola oil
½ tsp. salt
½ tsp. pepper
2 tbsp. sliced green onions
1 cup red cabbage, shredded
1 cup green cabbage, shredded
sliced carrots to taste
¾ cup dried cranberries

Mix and chill for 4 hours.

Oriental Slaw

1 lb. (1/2 head) cabbage, shredded
1 pkg. oriental flavor Ramen noodles,
    uncooked and broken
1 bunch green onions, chopped
1/3 cup slivered almonds, toasted
¼ cup sugar
1 pkg. oriental Ramen noodle seasoning
¼ cup oil (canola or sesame work well)

    Add ingredients to the cabbage in the order listed. Mix well and refrigerate 1 – 2 hours. Will keep in refrigerator, though noodles soften somewhat.

Avocado with Marinated Shrimp

½ cup oil
2 tbsp. vinegar
½ tsp. dill seed
dash cayenne pepper
1 lb. shrimp, peeled, deveined, and cooked
Boston Bibb lettuce
½ cup lime or lemon juice
1 ½ tsp. salt
½ tsp. dry mustard
1 tsp. capers
3 - 4 avocados, peeled and halved

    Prepare shrimp. Combine for marinade: oil, lime or lemon juice, vinegar, seasonings, and capers. Toss with cooked shrimp and chill for several hours, stirring occasionally. Brush avocados halves with marinade. Arrange avocados on lettuce leaves and fill with shrimp. Serve with remaining marinade. Serves 6 – 8.

Oriental Salad

1 package Ramen noodles, oriental flavor
¾ cup celery, diced
½ tsp. salt
¼ cup white vinegar
½ cup salad oil
1 small head cabbage

4 green onions, diced
¼ cup sunflower seeds
¼ cup cashews
¼ cup almonds, slivered
1/8 cup sesame seeds
1 tbsp. butter

Dressing: Mix contents of the seasoning packet from the Ramen noodles, salt, vinegar, and oil. Set aside.

Brown nuts and seeds in butter. They will burn easily so watch them very carefully. Slice the cabbage as thin as possible. Mix together the cabbage, onions, and celery. Add the nuts and ramen noodles that have been crumbled. Pour dressing over all and toss.

Orange and Spinach Pasta Salad

1 pkg. plus 1 tsp. orange drink mix (Kool-Aid, Tang, etc.)
½ cup oil
½ cup orange juice
¼ tsp. fennel seeds
2 cups bowtie pasta, cooked
3 cups torn raw spinach
2 medium oranges, peeled and cut into pieces
OR 1 can mandarin oranges
¼ cup green onion, sliced

Mix the first four ingredients in a jar and shake. Set aside. Put bowties in a bowl and add the spinach, oranges, and green onion. Just before serving, pour liquid mixture over the pasta in the bowl and toss.

Gold Rush Salad

1 head California iceberg lettuce, finely shredded (1½ quarts)
2 tbsp. olive oil
1 lb. boneless beef sirloin or chuck steak, cut into strips
1 small onion, chopped
2 tbsp. flour
1 tbsp. minced garlic (about 6 medium cloves)
1 tbsp. curry powder
½ to 1 tsp. crushed red pepper
1 cup white wine
½ cup water
½ cup chopped peanuts, or pine nuts
1 cup quartered cherry tomatoes

Heat oil in a large skillet until very hot. Add beef and onion all at once and sauté over high heat for 3 minutes or just until seared on outside. Mix in flour, garlic, curry, red pepper and salt to taste; then add wine and water. Cook, stirring until thickened. Line salad bowl with shredded Iceberg lettuce. Pour hot beef and sauce into lettuce and sprinkle with peanuts and tomatoes. Toss well and serve promptly. Serve with chutney if you like.

Oriental Chicken Salad

1 package Ramen noodles,
   oriental or chicken flavor
3 to 4 cups cabbage, shredded
4 green onions, chopped
1 small can water chestnuts,
   drained and sliced
½ cup toasted slivered almonds
1 cooked chicken breast, diced

Dressing:
3 tbsp vinegar
1/3 cup oil
2 tbsp sugar
¼ cup soy sauce (lite)
1 package Ramen noodle seasoning
sunflower seeds (optional)

In a large bowl, combine noodles, cabbage, onions, water chestnuts, almonds, and chicken. To make dressing, pour all ingredients into a jar, cover and shake well. Pour dressing over salad and chill until serving time. Top with sunflower seeds.

Chicken Salad

This recipe came from Greenley's Restaurant in Evansville, Indiana, where I met my husband. We both worked there while attending college.

6 boneless, skinless chicken breasts
poultry seasoning
2 tbsp. wine vinegar
1 tsp. coarse black pepper
1 red bell pepper, chopped
¼ cup minced onion
½ cup mayonnaise
½ cup frozen peas

Wash and dry chicken breasts. Simmer with poultry seasoning in water to cover until done. Drain, cool, and cut in ½" cubes. Add wine vinegar. Toss bell pepper and onion with black pepper. Toss with chicken cubes and add mayonnaise. Chicken pieces should just be coated with mayo. Rinse peas and add to salad. Chill for 1 hour or more to blend flavors. Very festive and healthy when served on a bed of leaf lettuce. Serves 4 – 6 people.

Ham & Sweet Potato Salad

This is a hit at the Golden Pioneer Museum's annual salad luncheon.

1 lb. sweet potatoes (2 medium),
   peeled and cut into 1" chunks
3 tbsp. grated fresh ginger
1/3 cup lime juice
2 tbsp. honey
1 tbsp. olive oil
1 tsp. Dijon mustard
¼ tsp. black pepper
2 pears (about 6 oz. each), peeled, cored,
   quartered lengthwise and sliced ¼" thick
½ lb. baked ham, cut into ½" chunks
1 red bell pepper, cut into 2" long matchsticks
½ cup thinly sliced red onion
6 cups torn Boston or leaf lettuce

In a medium pot of boiling water, cook potatoes for 12 minutes or until tender. Meanwhile, working over a large bowl, squeeze the ginger with your fingers to extract the juice; discard the solids. Whisk in lime juice, honey, oil, mustard, and pepper. Drain the potatoes well, add to bowl with lime juice mixture, toss to coat. Add the pears, ham, bell pepper, and onion, and toss again. Serve on a bed of lettuce. Serves 4

Boiled Dressing Salad

2 tbsp. flour
7 tbsp. sugar
2 eggs
½ tsp. prepared mustard
1 20 oz. can pineapple chunks, drained; use
    juice in dressing

2 tbsp. butter or margarine
2 bananas, sliced
1 10 oz. can mandarin oranges, drained
1 10 oz. jar maraschino cherries, drained
1 cup miniature marshmallows
apples or nuts (optional)

To make dressing, mix flour and sugar in pan. Beat eggs in a small bowl and add mustard and pineapple juice. Add the liquid to the flour and sugar and mix well. Cook about 10 minutes or until thick, stir while cooking. Add butter and set aside to cool.

Place the pineapple, bananas, oranges, cherries and marshmallows in a bowl, add cooled dressing and mix until fruit is covered. Chill 2 - 3 hours. Serves 6.

Note: For added flavor, dip apples and bananas in lemon juice.

Spinach Salad

1 10 oz. bag spinach, washed, dried and
    torn in pieces
1 8 oz. can water chestnuts, drained and sliced
1 16 oz. can bean sprouts, drained
8 or more strips bacon, fried, drained and
    crumbled
4 or more hard cooked eggs, peeled and sliced

1 cup vegetable oil
¾ cup sugar
1/3 cup ketchup
¼ cup vinegar
½ tsp. salt
1 medium onion
2 - 3 tbsp. Worcestershire sauce

In large bowl toss together spinach, bean sprouts, water chestnuts, bacon and eggs. In blender or food processor mix vegetable oil, sugar, ketchup, vinegar, salt, onion and Worcestershire sauce.

Mix about half of the dressing with spinach mixture or serve dressing on the side.

The Main Event

Throughout the years of the Colorado gold and silver booms, Golden served as the gateway to the mining districts. Railcars filled with all the wealth of the mountains flowed through the heart of the little town. Businesses of all types, including smelters, brickyards, paper mills, flour mills, and, of course, saloons, sprang up to meet the needs of the thousands of fortune-seekers and their families seeking wealth and a new life. Today Golden is still a vibrant community making significant contributions to the world's economic and scientific stage. The Colorado School of Mines, the National Earthquake Center, the National Renewable Energy Lab, CoorsTek, and the Coors Brewing Company are all headquartered in Golden.

(Photo: Birdseye map of Golden, 1873; courtesy of the Golden Pioneer Museum)

Prakes (Stuffed Cabbage)

1 head cabbage
1 ½ lbs. top rib roast
1 onion
1 15 oz. can whole tomatoes
1/3 cup honey
½ cup brown sugar
1 tbsp. salt
¼ tsp. pepper
juice of 1 lemon
1/3 cup golden raisins

Filling:
1 lb. ground beef
1 small onion, grated
¼ cup uncooked rice
2 eggs

Core the cabbage and parboil for a few minutes. Cut top rib into small pieces and place evenly in a roaster along with tomatoes, onion, honey, brown sugar, salt, pepper, lemon juice, and raisins. In a bowl combine ingredients for the filling. Remove the cabbage leaves and place a small patty of the hamburger filling into the thick end of each leaf. Fold each side over and roll up. Distribute each roll in the roaster evenly. Place into 325° oven, making sure there is enough liquid to cover the cabbage rolls. If there is not enough add boiling water to cover. Roast, covered, for 4 hours, basting at intervals.

Flank Steak Marinade

½ cup salad oil
¼ cup soy sauce
1 1/3 tbsp. Worcestershire sauce
2 2/3 tbsp. red wine vinegar
2 tsp. dry mustard
1 scant tsp. salt

1 tsp. freshly ground black pepper
2 tbsp. fresh lemon juice
¼ tsp. garlic powder
½ tsp. parsley flakes

Mix all ingredients well together. Trim all visible fat from flank steak and marinate steak in non-aluminum pan 12 – 24 hours in the refrigerator, turning halfway through. Grill outside, turning and basting frequently with marinade. To serve, slice meat thinly on the diagonal. It's really best rare to medium rare. The quantity of this marinade will generally be enough for two flank steaks. Serves about three people per pound of meat.

Mom's Barbecued Beef

3 – 5 lb. boneless cross rib roast
2 cloves garlic finely chopped
¾ cup water
¼ cup vinegar
2 tsp. brown sugar
2 tsp. chili powder

1 large onion, finely chopped
1½ cups catsup
¼ cup Worcestershire Sauce
2 tsp. salt
2 tsp. dry mustard
¼ tsp. Liquid Smoke

In a large Dutch oven, mix all ingredients except roast and cook on medium heat and bring sauce to the bubble. Reduce heat to low. Place 3 – 5 lb. roast in sauce, turning once to coat with sauce. Cover and cook slowly. Turn meat occasionally. Allow 2½ - 3 hours for a 3 – 4 lb. roast or 3 – 3½ hours for a 4 – 5 lb. roast. This may be done in the oven at 325° for 5 hours if you prefer.

Let meat cool about 15 minutes before slicing thinly across the grain. Return meat to sauce and keep warm. Serve as BBQ sandwiches on hot buttered sandwich rolls or sliced with sauce spooned over meat.

3 lb. roast serves 12 as sandwiches.

5 lb. roast serves 24 as sandwiches.

Barbecued Beef Brisket

5-6 pound beef brisket
3 oz. bottle liquid smoke
18 oz. bottle barbeque sauce (use your favorite)
celery salt

onion salt
garlic salt
black pepper

DAY ONE:

Put meat in heavy foil and pour liquid smoke over. Sprinkle generously with three salts and black pepper. Seal and refrigerate overnight.

DAY TWO:

Bake sealed meat for 5 hours at 250°, then open foil and pour barbeque sauce over and bake another hour. Refrigerate.

DAY THREE:

Slice cold brisket thinly and return to foil and sauce. This recipe will hold for days or can be frozen at this point. To serve, heat in 350° oven for one hour.

Italian Style Meat Loaf

1 pound ground beef
1 cup bread crumbs
1 onion, finely chopped
3 tbsp. parmesan cheese
1 egg
1 tsp. salt
¼ tsp. pepper
1 small can tomato sauce or 4 ounces salsa
1 tsp. oregano

Mix all except tomato sauce and oregano. Form into loaf and place into greased loaf pan. Bake at 350° for 30 minutes. Remove from oven, top with tomato sauce and oregano. Bake another 20 minutes or until the beef is cooked through.

Grilled Cedar Plank Steak With Blue Cheese

Untreated cedar fence slats make excellent grilling platforms; just cut to the length of your grill. Be certain to always soak the plank before using.

1 lb. boneless beef top sirloin steak, cut 1" thick
¼ cup olive oil
¼ cup dry red wine
3 cloves garlic, minced
1 tsp. ground pepper
½ tsp. salt
½ tsp. Dijon mustard
¼ cup green onion, sliced
¼ cup blue cheese, crumbled
2 tbsp. goat cheese (chevre)

Soak cedar plank in a container of clean water for at least three hours.

Trim fat from meat. Place in zipper seal bag. Stir together olive oil, red wine, two cloves garlic, pepper, salt, and mustard. Pour over steak. Close bag. Marinate from 6 to 24 hours in refrigerator, turning occasionally.

Set gas grill to medium heat, or prepare charcoal grill for medium heat. Drain steak, discard marinade. Remove cedar plank from water, drain but do not dry. Place cedar plank on grill rack, place steak on plank. Grill to desire doneness (10 minutes for medium rare). Meanwhile, in a small bowl combine green onions, one clove garlic, and cheeses.

When meat is done, transfer to serving platter, slice portions off across the grain. Serve with a dollop of cheese mixture over the top.

Jefferson Symphony Orchestra

*1801 Jackson Street
Golden CO 80401
Mailing Address:
PO Box 546, Golden CO
80402-0546 303.278.4237*
www.jeffersonsymphony.org

The Jefferson Symphony Orchestra began as a small community ensemble in 1953. It has grown into a 95-piece community orchestra in its truest sense. Bankers, teachers, company owners, ranchers, engineers, physicians, pilots, students and retired people all perform side-by-side in the JSO.

Roast Beef and Buttermilk Dumplings

1 cup buttermilk
1 tsp. baking soda
½ tsp. salt
flour
5 to 6 pound beef roast – season to personal taste

Fold in enough flour to make a fairly stiff dough that can be dropped from a spoon.

Roast the beef in the oven until tender at 350°. Drop dumplings on top of roast to cover it. Place roaster cover over roast and dumplings in the oven and bake additional 20 to 25 minutes.

Veal Forestier

1 ½ - 2 lbs. veal scaloppini, ¼" thick, cut into 2" pieces	salt to taste
	pepper to taste
garlic powder	1/3 cup dry vermouth
flour	1 tsp. fresh lemon juice
¼ cup butter or margarine	parsley to taste
½ - 1 lb. fresh mushrooms, thinly sliced	

Sprinkle veal pieces with flour and garlic. Heat butter in skillet. Sauté meat until golden brown on both sides. Heat mushrooms on top of meat, sprinkling with salt, pepper and vermouth. Cook covered over low heat for 20 minutes or until veal is fork-tender and mushrooms look done. (Check periodically and add water, if necessary, to keep meat moist.) To serve, sprinkle with lemon juice and parsley. Very good with mixed wild and white rice. Serves 6.

Colorado Casserole

1 pound lean ground beef
1 cup uncooked instant rice
½ cup green olives, sliced
1 can (28 oz.) chopped tomatoes
1 green pepper, diced
1 medium onion, sliced
2 tbsp. olive oil
salt to taste
2 tsp. chili powder (or to taste)
ground black pepper

Preheat oven to 350°. Sauté onions and green peppers in olive oil until golden brown. Add beef and stir until separated and browned. Mix rice into mixture and add tomatoes, green olives, and seasonings. Simmer 10 minutes. Pour into casserole and bake 45 minutes, stirring once or twice and adding tomato juice or water if mixture seems too dry. Serves 4.

Jefferson Symphony Orchestra

Continued

One of the few volunteer orchestras in the Front Range, the JSO continues the tradition of bringing classical and pops concerts to Jefferson County via a five-concert regular season, October through May, and several free concerts in the parks each August.

Regular concerts take place Sunday evenings in the Green Center on the Colorado School of Mines campus in Golden. In addition to the concerts, educational activities include in-school programs, pre-concert performances showcasing student groups, the annual Young Artists Competition each January, with prizes and scholarships.

Howdy Folks! Casserole

3 pounds lean ground beef
1 large onion, chopped
2 tbsp. butter
1 clove garlic, minced
salt
pepper
1 16 oz. can spaghetti sauce
    with mushrooms
1 10 oz. can tomatoes
3 tbsp. Worcestershire
1 tbsp. sugar
1 12 oz. pkg. egg noodles
1 pint sour cream
1 8 oz. pkg. cream cheese
Parmesan cheese

Preheat oven to 350°. Cook noodles in salted boiling water. Sauté onion and garlic in butter. Add ground beef and season with salt and pepper. To the onion and ground beef mixture, add the spaghetti sauce, tomatoes, sugar, and Worcestershire sauce. In the blender mix together cream cheese and sour cream. Reserve.

Put a small amount of meat in the bottom of a large casserole dish. Place all of the drained noodles over this. Next, pour all of the sour cream-cream cheese mixture over the noodles. Add the remaining meat sauce. Sprinkle with parmesan. Bake 45- 50 minutes or until bubbly. Serves 10 – 15 and can be frozen.

Tacorito

This Colorado favorite comes from the Holly West Restaurant in Applewood.

1 small onion, chopped
1 lb. ground beef
chili powder
salt and pepper
salsa
1 can cream of mushroom soup
garlic
milk
oregano
cumin
chopped chili
6 flour tortillas
cheese, grated

Sauté one small chopped onion. Add one pound ground beef; brown and drain. Add one minced garlic, one tablespoon chili powder, salt and pepper, and a little salsa. In a saucepan put one can of cream of mushroom soup, ½ cup milk, ¼ cup of salsa, ½ teaspoon oregano, ½ teaspoon cumin, and 2 tablespoons chopped chili. Simmer for 10 minutes.

Take 6 flour tortillas, place one in each of 6 au gratin dishes, add 1/6th of the beef to the tortilla, roll tortilla over and top with grated cheese. Bake at 350 ° for 20 minutes, or until it is hot and bubbly.

Garnish with chopped lettuce, chopped tomatoes, and pass with sour cream, guacamole, olives, and salsa.

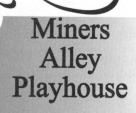

Miners Alley Playhouse

1224 Washington Avenue,
Suite 200
Golden, CO 80401
303.935.3044
www.morrisontheater.com

In June 2003, the Morrison Theatre moved to Golden, taking the space above Historic Foss Drug. The new Miners Alley Playhouse conducts classes, workshops, art shows, movie nights, music nights, and of course mainstage productions year-round. A beautiful lobby features a wine and beer bar, making the experience for patrons most enjoyable.

Lasagna

1 lb. ground meat (beef, turkey, or mixture)
garlic powder
1 pkg. spaghetti sauce mix
1 small (6oz.) can tomato paste
1 small (8 oz.) can tomato sauce
1 small (16 oz.) can tomatoes
13 lasagna noodles (about 11 oz.)
12 – 16 oz. ricotta or cottage cheese or a mixture
12 oz. (3 cups) mozzarella cheese
several tablespoons grated Parmesan

Bring to a boil a large pot of salted water. In a preheated skillet, brown meat, sprinkling with some garlic powder. When browned, drain any fat, sprinkle with spaghetti sauce mix and stir well. Add tomato sauce, paste, and tomatoes, stirring well and breaking up the tomatoes with a spoon. Add a little extra water (4-6 oz. depending on thickness). Cover and simmer for 20 minutes, stirring occasionally and adding more water if it seems too dry.

Meanwhile cook the lasagna noodles according to package directions (about 12 minutes). Drain well, rinsing in cold water.

Spread a very small amount of sauce mix in the bottom of a lasagna pan 10½" x 13". This will keep the noodles from sticking too much. Start layering the lasagna ingredients into the pan. There will be four sets of layers altogether. First, three noodles, then 1/4th of the mozzarella, then a tablespoon of Parmesan sprinkled over the top. Repeat three more times, ending with a more generous layer of Parmesan.

Cook the lasagna uncovered for about 30 minutes in a preheated oven at 325°. You know when it's done because it will smell delicious and will be bubbling around the edges at least.

Sloppy Joes (Steamburgers)

4 lbs. ground beef
1½ tbsp. onion
2 tsp. sugar
1 tsp. pepper
salt to taste
2 tsp. chili powder

2 tsp. vinegar
2 tsp. mustard
6 – 8 dashes Worcestershire sauce
1 cup ketchup
2 cans chicken gumbo soup

Brown ground beef, mix all ingredients in small bowl and add to ground beef. Simmer or put in crock-pot. Serve on buns or your favorite rolls.

Coors Rib-Eyes with a Soy-Ginger Marinade

1/2 cup soy sauce
1/4 cup maple syrup
6 cloves garlic, minced
1 tbsp. grated fresh ginger
1 tsp. mustard powder

1/2 tsp. sesame oil
1/4 tsp. hot pepper sauce
1/2 cup Coors Banquet beer, flat
4 beef rib eye steaks

In a medium size mixing bowl, combine soy sauce, pancake syrup, chopped garlic, grated ginger root, sesame oil, Tabasco sauce, and mix well to blend. Add beer and stir lightly to mix.

Prepare steaks by scoring any fatty outside areas on steak with a knife and gently poking a few holes into both surfaces. Place steaks in a zipper close plastic bag and pour marinade into bag. Marinate in the refrigerator for at least 1 hour or as long as overnight.

Preheat charcoal or propane grill to high. Place steaks directly on grill and sear one side for about 15 seconds. Turn steaks over and cook for about 5 minutes, then turn over and cook for another 5 minutes for medium-rare, depending on thickness, 2 minutes longer for medium, and so on.

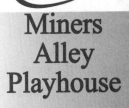

Miners Alley Playhouse

Continued

Our mission has been and will always be an educational and experience oriented arts organization, dedicated to providing opportunities for actors, directors, writers, designers, and technicians to gain valuable experience in a positive and supportive environment. Committed to arts education for children, the Theater has performed over 40 children's plays from the popular book KIDZeye Theater, which was co-published by the Theater. Acting for the Ageless brings improvisation and acting exercises to the senior population. Contact the Theater for production schedule, dates, and times.

Kraut Burgers

Quick Roll Dough:
2 cups warm water
1/3 cup sugar
2 pkgs. rapid rise yeast

1 tsp. salt
2 cups plus 4 cups flour
2 eggs
½ cup melted butter

Combine warm water with sugar and yeast. Stir until dissolved. Add salt and 2 cups flour. Beat 2 minutes with electric mixer. Add eggs and melted butter. Beat 1 minute more. Work in 4 cups flour. Turn out on board sprinkled with ½ cup flour and knead about 15 times. Put in greased bowl and cover. Let rise, then punch down. Take a small piece of dough and roll thin, until about 6" x 6". Enough dough for 2 dozen burgers.

Kraut Burger Filler:
2 tbsp. vegetable oil
2 large onions
2 ½ lbs. ground beef
2 – 3 tbsp. beef bouillon
1 pkg. Lipton dry onion soup
2 medium heads cabbage, shredded
Sauté onions in oil until done. Add ground beef and cook until brown. Add onion soup mix and beef bouillon. Slowly add cabbage and cook until done.

Preheat oven to 350°. Grease a cookie sheet. Be sure the dough has been rolled thin. The dough will rise when baked so if the dough is rolled out thin the burgers will not turn out to be all dough and not enough of the great filler. Spoon the filler onto the center of a rolled out piece of dough. Fold edges over and seal, using egg whites if necessary to seal edges. You want the dough to seal the filler inside the burger or some will leak out. Bake in oven for about 10 minutes, or until browned.

After they cool a little, pick one up, and enjoy every bite. They also freeze well, so when you have an overwhelming craving for a Kraut Burger you can just take one from the freezer and pop it into the microwave oven for about 2 minutes and be satisfied.

Movie Night Pizza

Crust:

4 cups flour

½ tsp. salt

1-10 cloves garlic

2 – 2 ½ cups of tepid water

2 tsp. sugar

2 packets of yeast

Blend flour, salt, and garlic in a mixer. Add sugar to warm water. Stir. Drop yeast on top of water, let sink down. Stir. Check for foam for positive reaction. Stir in with flour mixture. Mix thoroughly. If dough sticks to side of mixing bowl, add more flour until it clings to mixing paddle. Pull out paddle. Let rise, covered, for approximately 1 hour in a warm location.

Sauce:

Use spaghetti sauce or 1 can of Herdez green (verde) salsa

Toppings:

Whatever you like. Try some combination of the following, sliced:

Tomato, tomatillos, Portobello mushrooms, zucchini, black olives, green chilies, bell peppers, cilantro, onions, garlic

Cheese:

1 pound mozzarella, shredded

1 wedge fresh parmesan, shredded

Alternatives: Add shredded cheddar, crumbled feta, crumbled blue cheese

Meat:

Add sliced pepperoni, or Canadian bacon, or Italian dry salami

Alternatives: add shrimp (1/2 lb. peeled and boiled in 1 can of beer) or scallops (also boiled in beer)

Preparation:

While dough is rising, cut vegetables and prepare cheese and meat. Preheat oven to 425°. When dough has risen, spoon out onto floured bread board. Flour hands, pound down and make into a circular pizza crust, either by throwing or spreading. Place crust on lightly olive oil greased pan, cookie sheet, or pizza pan. Add spaghetti sauce or salsa. Spread over crust with the back of a spoon. Add a layer of mozzarella, but do not use all. Add a base layer of tomatoes or tomatillos and the rest of the vegetables. Add in some mozzarella and parmesan. Add meat of choice. Pizza will be large. Bake for 25 minutes. Look at periodically. Done when cheese is brown and bubbly. Cool slightly before cutting and serving. Serves 4 – 8.

Stuffed Chicken Breasts with Artichoke Hearts and Feta Cheese

2 tsp. olive oil
1 jar marinated artichokes, chopped
¼ cup minced shallots (about 3)
¼ cup crumbled feta cheese
1 tsp. dried Herbes de Provence, divided
¼ tsp. salt, divided
¼ tsp. black pepper
4 (4 oz.) skinned, boned, halved
    chicken breasts
1 cup chicken broth
2 tbsp. fresh lemon juice
2 tsp. cornstarch
chopped fresh parsley (optional)
lemon rind strips (optional)

    Drain and save marinade from artichokes. Chop artichokes and shallots. Heat 1 tsp. olive oil and saved artichoke marinade in non-stick skillet over medium heat. Add artichokes and shallots; sauté 4 minutes. Remove from pan; cool. Stir in cheese, ½ teaspoon Herbes de Provence, 1/8 teaspoon salt, and 1/8 teaspoon pepper.

    Cut a horizontal slit through thickest portion of each chicken breast half to form a pocket. Stuff 2 tablespoons of artichoke mixture into each pocket.

    Heat 1 teaspoon oil in a large non-stick skillet over medium heat. Add chicken, and sprinkle with 1/8 teaspoon salt, and 1 teaspoon pepper. Sauté 6 minutes on each side or until done. Remove from pan and keep warm. Add ½ teaspoon Herbes de Provence and broth to pan. Bring to a boil. Combine lemon juice and cornstarch. Add to broth mixture, stirring with a whisk. Cook 1 minute or until thick. Return chicken to pan. Cover and cook 2 minutes or until thoroughly heated. Garnish with parsley and lemon strips, if desired. Yield: 4 servings.

    For a nice addition, add ½ cup sliced mushrooms to artichoke mixture while sautéing.

Chicken Enchiladas

Sauce:
4½ tbsp. oil
2¼ tbsp. chili powder
2¼ tbsp. flour
½ tsp. salt
¾ tsp. onion powder
3/8 tsp. oregano
1½ tsp. vinegar
2¼ cup water
1 dozen corn tortillas

Filling:
1 can spicy refried beans
½ onion, finely diced
slices of cooked chicken breast
2 cups grated Monterey Jack cheese
Pace Picante Sauce
1 cup cottage cheese
2 cups grated cheddar cheese

Prepare sauce: Mix all the ingredients, except the water, together in saucepan. Then add water and bring to a boil. Simmer on medium heat until it thickens, stirring often. Set aside.

Preheat oven to 350º. To assemble enchiladas: Butter glass baking dish 13" x 10". Dip a corn tortilla in the sauce coating both sides, pull across the lip of pan to remove excess sauce, lay tortilla in bottom of buttered dish. Fill each tortilla with desired amount of each filling item. Fold both edges to the middle and place the rolled tortilla seam side down in dish. Continue until you have done 11 tortillas, fitting them into the dish. Tuck any remaining beans, onions, chicken in the edges of the enchiladas. Pour remaining sauce over the top and around the edges. Cover with ¼ cup grated cheese. Cover loosely with foil and bake for 30 minutes. Enchiladas are done when sauce is bubbling. Serve with lettuce, tomato, avocado, extra cheese and tortilla chips. Serves 6.

Chicken Pot Pie

1 whole chicken
1 cup celery
½ cup onion
4 tbsp. butter or margarine
¼ cup flour
1 tsp. salt

¼ tsp. pepper
2 cups chicken stock
2/3 cups cream or canned condensed milk
1 ½ cups cooked peas
1 ½ cups cooked carrots

Boil whole chicken with celery and onion. Take meat off of bone and reserve broth with celery and onion for use in sauce. Melt butter and remove from heat. Blend in flour and seasonings. Stir in chicken, chicken broth with celery and onion, and cream. Bring to a boil, stirring constantly. Boil one minute and then add cooked peas and carrots to the thickened sauce. Place prepared ingredients in a casserole dish and prepare buttermilk biscuit recipe below.

Buttermilk Biscuits

2 cups flour
2 tsp. baking powder
1 tsp. salt
¼ tsp. baking soda
1/3 cup oil
2/3 cup buttermilk

Mix flour, baking powder, salt, and baking soda in a bowl. Measure oil and buttermilk. Add to dry mixture. Stir with a fork until mixture cleans side of bowl and forms ball. Turn out onto a slightly floured counter. Knead a few times. Roll out to fit the size of casserole dish used for the pot pie mixture. Place biscuit dough on top of prepared ingredients in the casserole dish. Bake at 425° for approximately 15 minutes.

Chili Relleno Casserole

½ pound ground turkey or chicken
1 cup chopped onion
1¾ tsp. ground cumin
1½ tsp. dried oregano
½ tsp. garlic powder
¼ tsp. salt
¼ tsp. pepper
1 (16 oz.) can fat-free refried beans
2 (4 oz.) cans whole green chilies, drained
and cut lengthwise into quarters
vegetable cooking spray

1 cup (4 ounces) shredded Colby-Monterey
Jack cheese blend
1 cup frozen whole kernel corn, thawed and
drained
1/3 cup all-purpose flour
¼ tsp. salt
1 1/3 cups skim milk
1/8 tsp. hot sauce
2 eggs, lightly beaten
2 egg whites

Cook ground turkey and onion in a non-stick skillet over medium-high heat until turkey is browned, stirring until it crumbles. Remove from heat; add cumin and next 5 ingredients to skillet. Stir well, and set mixture aside.

Arrange half of green chili quarters in an 11" x 7" x 1½" baking dish coated with cooking spray; top with half of cheese. Spoon bean mixture in mounts onto cheese, and spread gently, leaving a ¼" inch border around edge of dish; top with corn. Arrange remaining chili strips over corn; top with remaining cheese. Set aside.

Combine flour and ¼ teaspoon salt in a bowl; gradually add milk and hot sauce, stirring with a wire whisk until blended. Stir in eggs and egg whites; pour over casserole. Bake, uncovered, at 350º for 1 hour and 5 minutes or until set; let stand 5 minutes. Cut into squares to serve. Serves 6.

Cornish Game Hens with Fruited Wild Rice

4 Cornish game hens
3 cups cooked wild rice (about ¾ cup uncooked)
2 small apples, cored and chopped (peel on)
¾ cup dried apricots, chopped
¾ cup walnuts, chopped
¾ tsp. dried ginger
¾ tsp. nutmeg
¾ tsp. salt
6 tbsp. butter, melted
apricot preserves (optional)

Thaw the hens, rinse well and pat dry.

Preheat oven to 350°. Combine the wild rice with the apples, apricots, walnuts, spices, and half the butter. Toss lightly to mix well. Stuff the hens with the rice mixture. Secure the openings with laces or skewers. Place any remaining stuffing in a small buttered, covered casserole. Place the hens in an open roasting pan, do not crowd them. Brush with some of the remaining butter. Bake hens and casserole dish of stuffing for one hour, basting hens with melted butter occasionally. Spoon the stuffing from the casserole around the hens and baste the hens with apricot preserves. Continue baking for another 15-20 minutes or until hens are nicely glazed and the stuffing lightly browned.

Serves 4 to 8.

Mitzutaki

This Japanese dish, sometimes called Shabu Shabu, is a healthy fondue perfect for parties. If you have leftover meat and vegetables, just add to remaining broth for a wonderful next-day soup. Feel free to substitute shellfish for any of the meat, and other types of vegetables such as green beans, baby corn, etc.

1 egg
2 tbsp white wine vinegar
¼ tsp dry mustard
1 cup oil
1/3 cup sour cream

2 tbsp. soy sauce
3 tbsp. dry sherry or rice whine
dash cayenne pepper

Combine egg, vinegar, and dry mustard in a blender. Blend on high, slowly drizzling in the oil, making a mayonnaise. Blend an additional 30 seconds. Add sour cream, soy sauce, sherry, and cayenne to blender and whir just to blend. Pour into serving bowls.

1 large can chicken broth
1 small can chicken broth
4 skinless chicken breasts, de-boned and sliced
1 small rump roast, thinly sliced
1 bunch spinach, washed
1 container medium tofu, diced into 1" cubes
½ lb. Chinese pea pods, ends trimmed

1 large package Chinese bean thread (cellophane) noodles
1 can sliced water chestnuts
1 can sliced bamboo shoots
1 lb mushrooms, washed and cut into bite size pieces
1 bunch green onions, cut into 1" lengths

Soak bean thread noodles for 30 minutes in hot water.

Place broth in an electric frying pan or fondue pot and heat. About 15 minutes before the meal, place chicken pieces in broth to cook. Clean, cut and place the vegetables on serving plates. At the meal, each person should thread a piece of meat or vegetable onto a bamboo or metal skewer and place into hot broth until cooked to desired doneness. Or, the vegetables can be added in small quantities to the broth and removed by each guest. Serve meat and vegetables with bean thread noodles and sauce. Serves 4.

Chicken Rice Dinner

8 to 12 chicken pieces (legs, thighs, breasts)
1 stick butter
1 can cream of mushroom or celery soup
1 can cream of chicken soup
1 to 1 ½ cups long grain rice
¾ can of water if mixture is too thick

Set oven to 350º. Melt butter in a 9" x 13" pan in the oven. When melted, add soup, rice, and water. Mix well. Lay chicken pieces on top of mixture. Bake in oven for one hour. Serves 6.

Chicken and Vegetables in Peanut Sauce

Chicken and Vegetables:
8 oz. skinned and boned chicken breast,
   cut into strips
1 tsp. cornstarch
1 tsp. peanut or vegetable oil
1 garlic clove, minced
1 medium red bell pepper,
   seeded and cut into thin strips
¼ cup water
1 tsp. teriyaki sauce

2 cups broccoli florets, blanched
dash each salt and pepper
Sauce:
¼ cup thinly sliced onion
1 cup water
1 packet instant chicken broth and seasoning
    mix
2 tbsp. peanut butter
1 tsp. teriyaki sauce

Sprinkle chicken with cornstarch. In 12" nonstick skillet, heat oil. Add garlic and chicken and sauté for 2 minutes. Add pepper strips, water, and 1 tsp. teriyaki sauce. Cook until pepper is tender-crisp, 2 – 3 minutes. Add broccoli, salt and pepper and cook until broccoli is thoroughly heated.

For sauce: In 8" nonstick skillet, cook onion over medium heat, stirring frequently, until translucent. Stir in water and broth mix and bring to a boil. Reduce heat, stir in peanut butter and teriyaki sauce, and let simmer until mixture is well blended. Serve over chicken and vegetables.

Chicken and Dumplings

Mom was one of 7 kids and she raised 5 of her own. Through this experience she learned the need for very simple, yet hearty meals that would stretch a dollar. This has been a family favorite for as long as I can remember.

2 – 3 lb. chicken pieces, skinned
1 pkg. dried onion soup mix
1 tbsp. paprika
3 cups water
cooking oil

Dumplings:

1½ cups flour
½ cup water
2 eggs
½ tsp. salt
¼ tsp. baking powder

Heat oil in deep kettle or Dutch oven. Brown chicken thoroughly. Sprinkle soup mix over chicken and toss, making sure each piece is covered. Allow to marinate for 5 minutes. Add 3 cups water and paprika, cover and simmer over low heat for 1 ½ hours. Add more water as necessary to keep chicken covered. Serves 4 – 6.

Dumplings:

Beat eggs. Add remaining ingredients and beat well. The dough should be rather fluffy. Remove chicken from the pot and place in warming oven. Bring the remaining broth to a slow boil. Drop dough by teaspoonful into the broth. It's best to only do a dozen or two at a time as they will clump together. Wait for dumplings to rise, then continue to cook for 2 more minutes. Remove cooked dumplings to a bowl and repeat the process until all of the batter is used. Double recipe if preparing more than 4 servings.

The Heart and Soul of Golden

When the Golden Cultural Alliance was formed, its purpose was to promote and protect the cultural and historic resources of Golden. The Heart and Soul celebration was born out of the need to inform Golden residents about all of these great organizations. February is Heart and Soul Month. To kick things off, the Alliance elects a Sweetheart Couple. The couple is chosen for their unwavering support of Golden and its cultural entities and exemplifies the spirit of "Heart and Soul."

Green Chili Chicken Delight

Green Chili
2 small (6 oz.) cans chopped green chilies
1 small onion, chopped
1 clove garlic, pressed
1 16 oz. can diced tomatoes
1 pound pork, cut into small pieces
salt and pepper to taste

Place ingredients in crock pot and cook all day at the low setting. Or, cook in saucepan on stove until pork pieces are tender and fully cooked.

Chicken
4 chicken breasts
4 slices mozzarella cheese

Broil chicken breasts until fully cooked and light brown. Melt cheese on each chicken breast. Serve 1 chicken breast over ½ cup cooked rice, smothered in green chili. Serves 4.

Sweet and Sour Lemon Herb Chicken

6 split skinless, boneless chicken breasts
2 ribs celery (with leaves), chopped
3 tbsp. olive oil
1 clove garlic, pressed or minced
1/3 cup lemon herb vinegar
1/3 cup honey

Preheat oven to 325º. Heat garlic and olive oil in skillet. Brown chicken. Place browned chicken in shallow baking dish. Distribute chopped celery atop chicken. Combine vinegar and honey, and then pour atop chicken. Bake uncovered 25 to 30 minutes or until chicken tests done. Garnish with sprig of lemon basil or lemon thyme.

Grilled Lime Chicken

1 ½ – 2 lbs chicken pieces
    per person
Lawrey's Seasoned Salt
paprika
lime juice

Choose whatever chicken pieces you prefer, skinned or unskinned, boned or unboned. Sprinkle them generously on both sides with Lawry's seasoned salt and paprika. Then place them in a single layer in a glass pan. Cover with lime juice. Marinate overnight, covered, in the refrigerator. Turn chicken in the morning. If the salt and paprika have worn off, sprinkle some more on. To grill: Mix a little melted butter with 1/4 – ½ cup lime juice. Grill 15 – 20 minutes, turning once and basting with lime juice.

The Heart and Soul of Golden

Continued

The Month carries on with nearly every organization hosting special events from free admission days, to theme exhibits, concerts, plays, etc. The Month concludes with two unique events. The Golden Landmarks Association hosts a Living Landmarks dinner, honoring members of Golden's community who have contributed to the history and preservation of the town. And last, but never least, is Buffalo Bill's Birthday Bash at the Buffalo Bill Memorial Museum - an event not to be missed!

Chicken and Sausage Jambalaya

Stock:
Boil 2 quarts water with:
1 large chopped onion
4 stalks celery, chopped
½ bunch shallots, chopped
1 tbsp. salt
¼ tsp. Tabasco
1 tsp. Accent seasoning

Boil for ten minutes, then add one medium-large chicken. Simmer on low boil until chicken is done, about 40 minutes. Remove and de-bone chicken. Strain and save stock.

Chop and simmer one pound of smoked sausage in a little water for 5 minutes. Allow the water to boil off. Remove sausage, keeping drippings in pan. Add to drippings and sauté:

1 cup finely chopped onion
¼ cup chopped green pepper
1 clove garlic, chopped
1 cup chopped celery
1 cup chopped shallots

Add:
1 16 oz. can tomatoes
2 cups uncooked rice
3 cups chicken reserved chicken stock
1 tsp. seasoned salt
¼ tsp. red pepper
¼ tsp. seasoned pepper
½ tsp. Accent seasoning
1 tbsp. Worcestershire sauce
½ tsp. Kitchen Bouquet
1 tbsp. sugar

Add chicken and sausage. Simmer over low heat until rice is soft, stirring occasionally. Add more broth if necessary.

Hot Turkey Salad

1 loaf Italian bread
½ cup chopped celery
¼ cup chopped green onions
¾ tsp. salt
½ tsp. curry powder
½ cup mayonnaise
2 cups turkey or chicken
½ cup shredded cheese

Cut loaf of bread in half lengthwise and hollow out each half. Mix together all ingredients except cheese and place in hollowed out bread. Place top half of loaf over lower filled half. Wrap in foil. Bake in 350º oven for 20 minutes. Unwrap, sprinkle with shredded cheese and return to oven for 5 minutes. Remove, cut into 1½ to 2 inch slices and serve.

Quiche Lorraine

10" pie shell, unbaked
6 slices bacon
10 thin slices Swiss cheese
4 eggs, lightly beaten
1 cup heavy cream
1 cup whole milk

1 tbsp. flour
ground nutmeg
cayenne pepper
black pepper
2 tbsp. diced onion

Bake shell at 400º for 10 minutes. Fry bacon until crisp. Drain. Sauté onions. Overlap bacon and cheese to cover bottom of crust. Add onion. In a separate bowl, combine eggs, cream, milk, flour with a pinch of nutmeg, a few grains of cayenne and black pepper. Pour custard mixture over bacon and cheese. Bake at 400° for 15 minutes and 325º for 30 minutes. If freezing, prepare fully and bake. Reheat a frozen quiche at 350° for 30 minutes.

Alternate: use 5 eggs and ¼ cup of Roquefort cheese in place of Swiss cheese.

Pork and Calypso Sauce

2 pound boneless pork tenderloin

Marinade:

½ cup soy sauce

2 tbsp. brown sugar

½ cup red wine

¼ cup vinegar

1 tbsp. chopped garlic

1 tbsp. grated ginger root

Calypso Sauce:

1 cup crushed pineapple

1 peeled, pitted and diced mango

½ cup sweet red pepper, diced

½ cup green onion, diced

1 tsp. finely chopped garlic

1 Anaheim green pepper,
    seeded and diced

Place the pork in a plastic bag with the marinade for several hours in the refrigerator. Two hours is best but one will do when you're running late.

Make up the Calypso Sauce just after you place the pork on the grill.

Grill the pork on a barbeque grill for at least ¾ hour. Start with the heat on high to brown the roast, then reduce the heat to be sure the meat is thoroughly cooked to an internal temperature of 170º. Let the roast rest for 15 minutes before placing on a plate. Slice the roast diagonally and spoon one-half of the sauce over the slices. Serve the remainder of the Calypso Sauce in a bowl for those who want more sauce on their meat.

Using a more piquant green pepper such as a jalapeno can increase the spiciness of the sauce should you wish. The mixture of sweet and spicy is great with pork!

Baked Pork Chops

4 thick pork chops (1" thick is nice)
salt
pepper
1 can cream of mushroom soup
1 cup milk

Preheat oven to 350°. Salt and pepper pork chops, then brown in skillet. Put chops into an ovenproof skillet. Blend together mushroom soup and milk and pour over the chops (soup mixture should cover the chops). If you need more liquid, add more milk or another can of soup.

Cook for two hours. Chops will be "fall apart tender" and the soup can be used as your gravy.

Melted Ham and Swiss Sandwiches

2 sticks margarine
1 onion, chopped
6 tbsp. mustard (any flavor)
6 tsp. poppy seed
buns
cooked ham
Swiss cheese

Sauté margarine, onion, mustard, and poppy seeds for about 10 minutes. Dip both sides of buns in mixture. Layer slices of ham and Swiss cheese on buns. Bake at 350° for 30 – 45 minutes.

Beer and Onion Pork Chops

4 pork chops, 1-2" thick, fat trimmed
salt
black pepper
2 tbsp. butter
2 tbsp. oil
1 large onion, sliced thin
1½ cups Killian's Irish Red beer
1 tsp. rosemary

Preheat oven to 325°. Season chops to taste with salt and pepper. In a large skillet, melt the butter and the oil. Over medium high heat, sear chops on both sides, just until browned but not cooked through. Remove from pan to a covered casserole dish. Pour off all but 1 tbsp. of fat from skillet. Add onion and cook until soft and translucent. Pour in beer and rosemary and bring to boil. Pour skillet contents over chops. Cover tightly and bake until tender, about 30 to 40 minutes depending on thickness of chops. To serve, remove chops to a warmed platter, strain liquid into a bowl, skim off fat, then pour over chops. Garnish with fresh rosemary.

Coors Glazed Ham

1 5 pound smoked ham, skin removed
½ cup fresh spinach leaves, diced
1¼ cups brown sugar
1 tsp. ground cloves
3 tsp. dry mustard
12 ounces Coors beer, flat
whole cloves

Preheat oven to 325°. Score fat into diamond shapes, and insert ½ tbsp. of spinach and a whole clove into center of each diamond. In a small bowl, blend brown sugar, ground cloves, mustard, and ¼ cup of beer. Rub into ham. Place ham into large baking dish. Bake for 20 minutes per pound, basting frequently with remaining beer. Serves 10.

Coors Ribs

4 pounds pork spareribs, cut into serving pieces
1½ cups Coors Banquet or Coors Light beer
½ cup honey
1 tbsp. lemon juice
1/4 tsp. cumin
3/4 tsp. cayenne
1/2 tsp. garlic powder
1 tsp. sage
1½ tsp. dry mustard
1 tsp. salt
½ tsp. fresh ground black pepper

   Place the ribs in a shallow pan. Mix remaining ingredients and pour over ribs. Marinate, covered, in the refrigerator for 24 hours, turning once to coat.

   Preheat charcoal or propane grill, allow to cool to low heat. Remove ribs from marinade, reserve liquid. Place onto grill, about 4 inches from heat. Cook, turning and basting with reserved liquid frequently, about 1¼ hours, or until brown. Can be baked in a preheated 350º oven for 1½ hours until brown and glazed, basting frequently. Serves 4.

   The Ribs go fabulously with the Three Grain Pilaf (Recipe on next page)

Three-Grain Pilaf with Dried Apricots & Cherries

¼ cup dried cherries
¼ cup dried apricots, diced
½ cup apple juice or apple cider
½ cup chopped onion (1 small onion)
1 tbsp. butter
1/3 cup millet
1/3 cup quinoa
1/3 cup bulgur wheat
3 cups chicken stock or broth

Note: Bulgur or bulgur wheat, most often used in tabouli salads, is available in supermarkets. Health-food stores carry millet, quinoa and dried cherries.

Combine the cherries and apricots with the apple juice or cider in a small saucepan. Cover and bring to a boil, then reduce the heat and simmer gently for about 10 minutes, or until the fruit has absorbed most of the liquid. Set aside.

Sauté the onion in the butter over medium-high heat for about 5 minutes, or until lightly browned. Add the millet, and cook 3 - 4 minutes longer. Stir in the quinoa, bulgur and chicken stock and bring to a boil. Drain the fruit and add it to the grains. Cover and bake in a 350° oven for 35 minutes. Remove from the oven. Let the pilaf sit, covered, for 5 minutes before serving. Serves 6 - 8.

Penang Shrimp Curry

4 oz. butter
1 clove garlic, crushed
1 onion, finely chopped
3 stalks celery
1 green pepper, seeded and chopped
1 carrot, chopped
2 tomatoes, peeled, seeded and chopped
1 tsp. parsley chopped
1 bay leaf, crumbled
dried thyme, a pinch
dried mint, a pinch

dried marjoram, a pinch
2 cloves
¼ tsp. dried basil
2 tbsp. flour
2 tbsp. curry powder
½ tsp. cayenne pepper
½ tsp. ground nutmeg
2 cups condensed consommé
1 cup dry white wine
2 lbs. freshly boiled and shelled shrimp

Melt butter in large saucepan. Add next 13 ingredients and cook until vegetables are soft. Then sprinkle in flour mixed with curry powder, cayenne and nutmeg; mix thoroughly with vegetables, stirring well, and cook for about 5 minutes. Slowly add the consommé. When the mixture begins to thicken, add the wine. Cook over low heat for about 30 minutes. Add the shrimp and let heat through; curry is now ready to serve.

Have on buffet table a large bowl of fluffy rice, the curry, and as many side dishes as you want. Essentials are unsweetened shredded coconut, finely chopped little green onions, chopped peanuts, finely chopped hard-cooked eggs, almonds or cashews, Major Grey's chutney and finely chopped orange peel. Also have on table chilled bottles of dry white wine and chilled bottles of beer or ale. Seedless raisins, diced dates, bananas are all nice. I cook shrimp in water with plenty of salt and bay leaf, carrot, celery and 1 cup wine added to cooking water.

Crab Casserole

2 cans crab meat
¼ cup butter
¼ cup green pepper sautéed
½ cup mayonnaise
1 egg, beaten
1 tbsp. parsley

2 tbsp. Worcestershire sauce
¼ cup cream
1 tsp. prepared mustard
¼ tsp. salt - pepper to taste
1/8 tsp. nutmeg
½ cup bread crumbs

Combine in casserole dish and bake at 350 degrees for 20 minutes.

Blue Moon Beer Battered Shrimp

2 pounds medium shrimp, deveined and peeled with tails left on
1 cup flour
2 tsp. salt
1 tsp. baking powder
½ tsp. cayenne pepper
¾ cup Blue Moon beer
½ cup milk
2 large eggs, beaten
3 cups vegetable oil

Butterfly shrimp by slicing most of the way through from back to front; press flat. Dry with paper towel. Stir together flour, salt, baking powder, and cayenne. Whisk in beer, milk, eggs. It will be foamy. Add shrimp and let stand for 30 minutes. Heat oil in a deep fryer to 365°. Remove shrimp 1 at a time from batter and fry in small batches, turning twice to ensure they are golden brown and crispy, about 4 minutes total. Using slotted spoon, remove from oil and dry on paper towels. Serve with cocktail sauce, or other favorite sauce.

Salmon with Tropical Salsa

Marinade:
4 - 6 oz. salmon filets
½ cup olive oil
juice of ½ lemon
3 garlic cloves, crushed
1 tbsp. shredded fresh cilantro
1 tbsp. ground cumin
pinch of cayenne pepper
salt and black pepper to taste

Combine the marinade in a shallow nonmetallic dish. Place the filets in the marinade, turning them to make sure they are coated. Then cover and leave in refrigerator overnight.

Salsa:
9 oz. can pineapple pieces, drained
1 small papaya (or mango), peeled, seeded and diced
1 small red bell pepper, cored, seeded and diced
1 small green bell pepper, cored, seeded and diced
2 tbsp. chopped fresh cilantro
1 tbsp. white vinegar

Combine salsa ingredients in bowl and set aside. Remove the salmon filets from the marinade and broil, placing approximately three inches from the heating element, for approximately 4 minutes on each side, until fish is opaque. Plate and serve with salsa on top.

Trout with Portobello Mushroom and Peppers

3 – 4 good sized fresh trout, heads and tails on, cleaned and rinsed; one per person
1 large Portobello mushroom (or two smaller ones)
1 yellow bell pepper
1 red bell pepper
olive oil
salt and pepper

Place the trout on large squares of aluminum foil drizzled with oil. Slice the peppers and the mushroom in long narrow slices and put inside and on either side of the trout. Lightly drizzle with more oil, and lightly salt and pepper. Wrap the foil into packets, and grill on each side for 4 – 5 minutes, turning several times. The trout is done when the eye of the fish turns opaque. The peppers will still be somewhat crisp. This recipe can also be adapted for cooking on a campfire over low coals, or baking in a 350° oven.

To serve, unwrap the packets and bone the trout in the foil. To bone, lift the tail and with a fork lightly poke through the skin and meat under the tail and separate the fillet downward from the bone all along the body to the head. Turn the trout and gently fillet the other side. You should end up holding a tail attached to the spine, rib bones and head. Plate it surrounded by mushrooms and peppers, or serve right in the foil if you're camping. Hint: the best part of a trout is a small round section of cheek right under the eye!

Trout with Bacon and Onion

This is a great recipe for people who think they don't like trout.

3 – 4 trout, cleaned and rinsed
2 slices of bacon per trout
1 large Maui or Vidalia (sweet) onion (or 2 smaller ones)
pepper

Place the trout on large squares of aluminum foil. Slice the onion into long narrow strips, and stuff into the trout. Place a slice of bacon on either side of the trout, wrap, and grill as above. The onions will still be somewhat crisp and the bacon lightly cooked when the trout is done. If you wish, you can cook longer until the bacon is medium done and the onions are soft without hurting the trout if you turn it every few minutes. This variation needs no salt, but you may wish to lightly pepper when serving.

Orange Salmon in Red Wine

1 ½ pounds salmon fillet
2 oranges, sliced thinly
¼ cup finely chopped fresh parsley
2 cups Merlot

Preheat oven to 350º. Place ½ of orange slices in bottom of 11" x 7" glass baking pan. Sprinkle 1/8 cup parsley over oranges. Place salmon fillet on top of orange slices. Arrange remaining orange slices over fillet and sprinkle with remaining parsley. Pour wine over salmon. Cover pan with foil and bake in 350° oven for 30 minutes or until done.

Baked Salmon in Newspaper

1 whole salmon, cleaned, head removed, skin on
1 fresh newspaper – 5 sheets*
cookie sheet
water

Preheat oven to 400° (410° above 5,000 feet). Make certain you know the weight of the salmon. Wash it thoroughly. Place on cookie sheet. Wet one sheet of newspaper, carefully to prevent tears. Wrap salmon in wet newspaper sheet. Wet a second sheet and third sheet and wrap salmon in them. Bake 10 minutes per pound of salmon.

Remove from open and place onto 2 remaining sheets of dry newspaper. The paper will be charred and dry. Slit oven newspaper along the cleaning slit of the fish. The skin will come off with the newspaper. Slice fillets along the ribs, then remove skeleton and slice bottom fillets.

*Preferably use a fresh newspaper with a liberal bent. If you're wondering why…Never use anything old, it should be preserved as historic…Liberals can enjoy that it was a right choice while conservatives can enjoy that the liberal paper is getting to smell like fish and is burned!

Southwest Pasta and Shrimp

8 large Roma tomatoes, cored and seeded
2 tsp. Kosher salt
½ tsp. fresh ground black pepper
1 pound uncooked fettuccine
1 tsp. crushed red pepper flakes
1 pound medium shrimp, peeled
   and deveined
8 tbsp. unsalted butter, cold
½ cup silver tequila
1 avocado, peeled and diced
1 bunch fresh cilantro, chopped

    In a food processor, or a blender, puree tomatoes until smooth, adding 1 – 2 tbsp. water if dry. Reserve. Fill a large pot with water and bring to boil. Add 1 tsp. salt and fettuccine and cook no longer than 8 minutes (al dente). Drain.

    While the pasta is cooking, melt 4 tbsp. butter in a large oven-safe skillet (not Teflon) over high heat. Sauté shrimp and remaining tsp. salt, pepper, and red pepper until shrimp are pink, about 1 minute per side. Add tequila and flambé (do this carefully). When flames have diminished, remove shrimp with a slotted spoon. Reserve. Add tomato puree to butter in pan and bring to boil. Cook until reduced by a third. Adjust seasoning to taste. Break apart remaining butter into small pieces and stir into sauce with shrimp. Stir till smooth. Remove from heat and ladle over bowls of fettuccine. Garnish with avocado and cilantro. Serve immediately.

Baked Scallops with Tomatoes

1/2 cup packed cut basil leaves
1 tbsp. minced fresh cilantro
2 tbsp. minced fresh parsley
1 tbsp. fresh minced oregano
1 tbsp. fresh minced chives
2 cloves garlic, minced
1½ lbs. sea scallops

Sauce:
juice of one fresh lime
2/3 cup olive oil
salt to taste
pepper to taste
2 – 3 large ripe tomatoes

Blend herbs, adding oil gradually. Drizzle a little on bottom of baking dish. Place scallops flat on bottom and season with salt and pepper. Slice tomatoes ¼" thick and layer over scallops. Spoon sauce over tomatoes. Bake in preheated 425° oven for 10 minutes. Serve with crusty bread.

Deviled Crab

1 small onion, minced
2 tbsp. flour
2 tbsp. butter
1 tbsp. lemon juice
1 tsp. Worcestershire sauce
dash cayenne pepper
½ cup cream or milk

1 can flaked crabmeat
    or frozen crab, thawed
1 cup buttered bread crumbs
¼ cup butter, melted
1 tbsp. parsley, chopped
1 hard boiled egg, chopped

Sauté onion in butter. Add flour, lemon juice, Worcestershire sauce, cayenne, parsley, and cream. Cook until smooth. Add crabmeat and egg. Fill individual ramekins or custard cups with mixture; top with bread crumbs, being careful to cover the edges. Pour butter on top. Bake at 350° for 30 minutes or until browned.

A Bountiful Harvest

Jonas and his son, Oscar, constructed the Rock Flour Mill in 1867. The flour was ground on stone burrs then screened through silk bolting cloth. Ole Swenson served as the millwright. Barber put in a narrow gauge line from the Colorado Central main line to his mill to facilitate the transfer of grain and flour. The Barbers closed the mill in the late 1880s when the Hungarian Flour Mill of Denver put in steel burrs for grinding, thereby making stone burrs virtually obsolete. One of the grinding stones from the mill was recovered by the Golden Landmarks Association and is on permanent display at the Golden Pioneer Museum.

(Photo: Rock Flour Mill, c.1880; courtesy of the Golden Pioneer Museum)

Corn & Bulgur Salad with Cilantro and Lime

½ cup bulgur
½ cup boiling water
1 tbsp. olive oil
3 ears of corn, shaved
salt to taste
½ cup red onion, diced
1 jalapeno, seeded and sliced thin
1 tbsp. lemon juice
1 tbsp. lime juice
cayenne pepper
1 tbsp. cilantro, chopped
1 tbsp. fresh sage, about 5 large leaves

Place bulgur in a medium bowl and pour boiling water over it. Cover and let sit for 20 minutes.

Meanwhile, heat the oil in a sauté pan. Add the corn and 1/3 tsp salt and cook over medium heat for 5 minutes. Add the onion and cook for 3 minutes or until the corn is tender. Allow to cool, then toss with the bulgur, jalapeno, lemon and lime juices, ½ tsp salt, and a few pinches of cayenne. Add salt if necessary. Toss in cilantro and sage just before serving.

Serves 4 to 6.

Herbed Spinach Bake

1 10 oz. package frozen chopped spinach
1 cup cooked rice
1 cup shredded sharp cheese
2 beaten eggs
2 tsp. soft butter
½ cup milk
2 tsp. chopped onion
½ tsp. Worcestershire sauce
1 tsp. salt
¼ tsp. rosemary or thyme

Preheat oven to 375º. Cook spinach and drain. Mix with all other ingredients. Pour into 10" x 6" x 2" baking dish. Bake for 20 – 25 minutes or until knife inserted in center comes out clean.

Rice and Walnut Loaf

2½ cups cooked brown rice
1 cup finely chopped walnuts
2/3 cup minced parsley,
2/3 cup minced green onion
1 4-oz. can chopped mild green chilies
1/3 cup melted butter
½ cup milk
2 eggs
1½ cups shredded sharp Cheddar cheese
1 tsp. leaf oregano
½ tsp. salt
freshly ground black pepper

Combine rice, nuts, parsley, onion and chilies. Mix together butter and milk and beat in eggs lightly. Stir into rice mixture with cheese, oregano, salt and pepper. Pack in a well-greased loaf pan and bake in a preheated 350° oven for 45 -50 minutes or until set. Serves 4 -5.

Vegetarian Sloppy Joes

1 cup dry lentils
2 ½ cups water
1/8 tsp. salt (optional)
½ cup onion, chopped
½ cup celery, finely chopped
½ cup green pepper, chopped
½ cup chili sauce
½ tsp. garlic powder
1½ to 2 tsp. chili powder

Place lentils in a pot with 2½ cups of water, salt (if desired), and onion. Bring to a gentle boil. Reduce heat to very low and allow to simmer until lentils are very tender (about 40 minutes). After about 20 minutes, add celery and peppers. Watch lentils so they don't become dry and burn. Add small amounts of water as needed during cooking time until the lentils soften. Add chili sauce, garlic powder, chili powder and an additional ¼ cup water (or enough to bring to desired consistency). Cook until it's desired thickness and tenderness. Serve on whole-grain buns. This recipe makes enough filling for 5 - 8 sandwiches.

Vegetable Loaf Italian Style

1 pound fresh spinach or 1 package (10 ounces) frozen spinach, thawed
3 tbsp. vegetable oil
2 cups diced zucchini
1 cup onions, chopped
½ cup celery, chopped
½ tsp. crushed garlic
3 eggs, lightly beaten
¾ cup Italian-style bread crumbs
¾ cup ricotta or cottage cheese
½ cup shredded mozzarella cheese
1 16 oz. jar spaghetti sauce

Preheat oven to 350°. Remove and discard stems from fresh spinach; wash thoroughly. With water clinging to leaves, place spinach in a saucepan with a tight-fitting lid; cover and cook until wilted, 2 - 3 minutes. Discard liquid, cool and chop spinach. Place in a strainer and press out as much liquid as possible. Or, place uncooked frozen spinach in a strainer; press out as much liquid as possible; set spinach aside. In a medium saucepan heat oil until hot. Add zucchini, onions, celery and garlic; sauté until vegetables are tender, about 10 minutes; set aside. In 2 large bowls mix eggs, bread crumbs, ricotta and mozzarella cheeses and reserved spinach; mix well. Stir in reserved vegetables. Turn into a greased and bread crumb-coated 8-inch loaf pan. Bake until golden, about 1 hour. Run a sharp knife around sides of loaf pan. Turn out onto plate, then reverse so that the golden side is up. Serve with hot spaghetti sauce along with sautéed mushrooms, if desired.

Egg & Mushroom Casserole

10 hard cooked eggs
2 3 oz. cans sliced mushrooms
milk
6 tbsp. butter or margarine
4 tbsp. all purpose flour

½ tsp. salt
½ tsp. onion salt
1 cup celery, chopped
1 cup packaged stuffing mix
1 cup grated American cheese

About 50 minutes before serving, slice eggs into casserole dish. Drain juice from mushrooms into 2 cup measuring cup; add milk to make 2 cups. Preheat oven to 375º. Melt butter or margarine in a saucepan over medium heat. Stir in flour, salt and onion until blended, stirring constantly until sauce is thickened. Add mushrooms and celery. Pour over eggs. Scatter stuffing mixed with cheese over top. Bake uncovered 20 minutes until bubbly.

Cheese Spinach Casserole

1 12 ounce carton creamed cottage cheese
3 eggs
¼ cup butter, cold
¼ pound cheddar cheese
1 pkg. frozen spinach
2 tbsp. flour
½ cup bread crumbs

Mix together cottage cheese, eggs, cheese, and butter until it forms coarse pieces. While spinach is still frozen cut into irregular pieces. Mix spinach into cottage cheese mixture and pour into greased casserole dish. Sprinkle with bread crumbs. Bake at 350º for about an hour. Serves 4 - 6.

Greek Tabbouleh

2 cups water
½ cup uncooked bulgur (tabbouleh)
2 tsp. cold-pressed olive oil
1 cup chopped spinach
½ cup tomato-basil or plain
    feta cheese, crumbled
½ cup mushrooms, sliced
½ cup canned kidney or black beans, drained

½ cup canned garbanzo beans, drained
½ cup canned artichoke hearts,
    drained and chopped
1½ tsp. basil
1 tsp. black pepper
½ tsp. oregano
2 garlic cloves, minced

Bring water to boil. In a medium bowl, combine basil, oregano, and bulgur. Pour hot water over bulgur and set aside for 30 minutes.

In a medium skillet, heat oil over medium-high heat. Add spinach and sauté just until wilted. Remove from heat. Combine bulgur, spinach, feta, and remaining ingredients in a large bowl. Cover and chill 1 hour. Looks lovely when served with a topping of tiny grape tomatoes and fresh sprigs of chives, oregano, or rosemary. About 5 side-dish servings.

Green Chile and Potato Casserole

6 potatoes, boiled and sliced thin
1 onion, diced
1 pint sour cream
1 can (4 oz.) chopped green chiles, drained (or jalapenos)
6 to 8 ounces Monterey Jack cheese, shredded
salt and pepper to taste
favorite salsa

Mix all ingredients together and pour into casserole dish. Bake at 350° for 30 minutes. Top with salsa of your choice.

Pea-Broccoli Casserole

This is a great Thanksgiving side dish!

1 pkg. (10 oz.) frozen peas
1 pkg. (10 oz.) frozen broccoli
or 1 pound fresh broccoli, chopped
1 small jar Cheez Whiz

or 4 ounces shredded cheddar cheese
½ can cream of mushroom soup
1 can French Fried Onions

Cook vegetables in water just enough to heat through. Drain and mix with Cheez Whiz and soup. Pour into casserole dish. Cover and bake at 350º for 25 minutes. Remove lid and top with a can of French Fried Onions. Bake 5 minutes more.

Vegetable Strata

1 - 1½ cups cauliflower (cut into bite-size pieces)
1 - 1½ cups broccoli (cut into bite-size pieces)
2 - 2½ cups cabbage (sliced thick, then chopped)
9 - 10 slices dried bread, cubed
OR 1 pkg. croutons
¾ cup grated cheddar cheese (divided)
9 - 10 eggs beaten with 3 cups milk
1 tsp. dry mustard

Boil vegetables separately until just tender. Set aside. Meanwhile, grease a 9" x 12" baking dish. Spread bread cubes on bottom to make a healthy layer. Sprinkle ½ cup cheddar cheese over cubes. Add mustard to beaten eggs. Pour over bread mixture. Drain vegetables and mix. Layer on top of bread, pressing into eggs. Let stand at least one hour in refrigerator. May be put together and refrigerated overnight.

Bake in 350º oven about one hour. Just before eggs are set, sprinkle cheese over top. Let stand 15 - 20 minutes before slicing into squares for serving.

Meatless Half-Hour Chili

This recipe was printed in The Denver Post Magazine supplement on September 27, 1992.

1 tbsp. oil
1½ onions, chopped
1 carrot, chopped
1 tbsp. minced jalapeno pepper
   (fresh or canned)
2 cloves garlic, minced
2 tsp. chili powder
1 28 oz. can and 1 14 oz. can tomatoes,
   chopped, with their juice
1 tsp. ground cumin
1 tsp. brown sugar
2 15 oz. cans red kidney beans,
   drained and rinsed
Optional: ½ cup bulgur
          ½ cup low-fat yogurt
          ½ cup chopped scallions
          ½ cup chopped fresh cilantro
            or parsley

In a Dutch oven or a large saucepan, heat oil over medium heat. Add onions, carrots, jalapenos, garlic, chili powder and cumin. Sauté for 5 – 7 minutes, or until the onions and carrots are soft. Add tomatoes with their juice and the sugar; cook for 5 minutes over high heat. Stir in beans and bulgur, and reduce heat to low. Simmer the chili, uncovered, for 15 minutes, or until thickened. Serve with yogurt, scallions and cilantro or parsley on the side. Cornbread is an excellent companion. Serves 4.

Roasted Asparagus with Sesame Seeds

1 tbsp. olive oil
2 lbs. fresh asparagus, trimmed
1 tbsp. coarse salt
3 – 4 tbsp. sesame seeds

Preheat oven to 425°. Lightly brush the oil over the asparagus, rolling them to distribute the oil evenly. Spread the spears in a single layer in a shallow pan and sprinkle with salt. Roast, uncovered, until the spears are just tender when pierced with the tip of a knife, about 10 minutes.

While asparagus is roasting, toast the sesame seeds in a dry skillet over medium heat, stirring constantly, until the seeds are golden and aromatic, about 2 – 3 minutes. Arrange asparagus on a serving plate and sprinkle with the toasted seeds.

Zuccanoes

4 medium zucchini
1 tbsp. olive oil
1½ cups onion, minced
1 tsp. salt
½ pound mushrooms, minced
6 cloves garlic, minced
1½ cups rice, cooked
1½ cups almonds, minced or ground

3 tbsp. lemon juice
black and cayenne pepper to taste
small handfuls of freshly minced herbs
    (i.e., parsley, basil, thyme, dill,
    chives, marjoram)
1 cup grated Swiss cheese (optional)
1 batch beet puree (optional)

Cut zucchini lengthwise down the middle. Use a spoon to scoop out the insides, leaving a canoe with ¼ inch shell. Finely mince the scrapings; set aside.

Heat the oil in a medium skillet. Add onion and salt and sauté over medium heat 5 to 8 minutes or until onion is soft. Add zucchini innards and mushrooms, sauté another 8 to 10 minutes. Add the garlic during the last few minutes.

Place rice and almonds in a medium bowl. Stir in the sauté and lemon juice; mix well. Season to taste with black pepper, cayenne, and fresh herbs.

Preheat oven to 350°. Fill zucchini shells with mixture, top with cheese if desired and bake 30 to 40 minutes until heated throughout. Serve hot, sublimely augmented by room temperature beet purée.

Serves 4 to 6

Beet Purée:

2 beets (2½ inch diameter)
½ cup apple or orange juice
2 tbsp. lemon juice

2 tsp. cider vinegar
2 tsp. honey
½ tsp. salt
black pepper to taste

Place beets in small saucepan of water and boil until tender, 20 to 30 minutes. Cool until comfortable to handle. Rub off skins and purée in a blender or food processor with the juices and vinegar. Transfer to a small bowl. Stir in honey, salt, and pepper. If necessary, thin to desired consistency with a little more fruit juice.

Spinach Lasagna

1 lb. ricotta cheese
1 egg
2 cups shredded mozzarella cheese
1 10 oz. pkg. frozen chopped spinach, thawed and drained
1 tsp. salt
1 tsp. dried oregano
1/8 tsp. pepper
4 cups spaghetti sauce
9 uncooked lasagna noodles

Preheat oven to 350º. Grease a 9" x 13" baking dish. In a large bowl, combine the ricotta cheese, egg, 1 cup mozzarella cheese, thawed and thoroughly drained spinach, salt, oregano, and pepper. In the prepared pan, layer one cup of the sauce. Top with 3 uncooked lasagna noodles and ½ of the ricotta mixture. Repeat with another layer of sauce, noodles, and ricotta mixture. Top with remaining noodles and sauce. Sprinkle with remaining mozzarella cheese. Cover tightly with foil. Bake for 1 hour and 15 minutes. Remove from oven and let sit 15 minutes before serving.

Golden Pioneer Museum

923 10th Street
Golden, CO 80401
303.278.7151
www.goldenpioneermuseum.com

Founded in 1938 as a W.P.A Project, the Golden Pioneer Museum is one of the oldest public museums in Golden. The Museum's collection covers a wide range of local history, beginning with the Native Americans and continuing through the 21st century. Some of the unique things visitors may enjoy include a velvet-covered piano, an 1860s pharmacy, Native American dolls, and vintage clothing.

Vegetarian Lasagna

It's healthier than the real thing and tastes great!

4 – 6 cups spaghetti sauce
1 1 lb. box of lasagna-style pasta noodles
1 large (24 oz.) carton of low fat (1%) cottage cheese
1 – 10 oz. package frozen chopped spinach, thawed
1 1-lb. bag grated mozzarella chest

Preheat oven to 350°. Assemble lasagna in a 9" x 13" pan as follows:

Ladle about 2 cups of sauce and spread over the bottom of pan. Cover sauce with a single layer of uncooked lasagna noodles (liquid absorbed during cooking will soften the noodles). Spread about 1½ cups cottage cheese over lasagna noodles. Sprinkle a generous amount of grated mozzarella cheese, covering the cottage cheese. Add all of the spinach, covering cheese layers. Repeat all layers except for spinach, ending with the mozzarella cheese (start by spooning the sauce right on top of the spinach). Bake for about one hour or until cheese is melted and nicely browned.

Penne al Boscaiolo

1 oz. package dried Porcini
mushrooms (do not substitute)
water
2 tbsp. white onion chopped
1 stick of butter
3 tsp. concentrated tomato
    paste in a tube

1 chicken bouillon cube
fresh parsley
½ - ¾ cup heavy cream
fresh parmigiano reggiano
1 lb. of penne pasta
salt and pepper to taste

Put the mushrooms in a pot with about 1 quart of water and bring it to a boil. When it boils, reduce the heat to very, very low and let the mushrooms soften (about 10 – 15 minutes). You can do this while you are preparing the other ingredients. The water should have turned a deep, mushroomy brown. Filter the mushrooms using a mesh strainer lined with paper towels. Reserve the liquid – you will use it in making the sauce. Pick the mushrooms off the towel and cut them into smaller pieces (not too small).

Melt the butter in a large non-reactive skillet and put in the onions. When the onions become translucent add the tomato paste and stir. Add a few ladlefuls of the mushroom liquid and the bouillon cube and let it reduce for about 20 minutes, stirring and making sure there is enough liquid. Add the cut up mushrooms and cook for 8 – 10 more minutes. Meanwhile, prepare pasta.

Add the heavy cream to the sauce and turn the heat up to a high for just a few minutes, being careful to stir so it doesn't stick or burn. Add the parsley and salt and pepper to taste (you won't need too much salt because the bouillon is salty). Throw the sauce on the cooled pasta and top with freshly grated parmigiano and Buon appetito!

Golden Pioneer Museum

Continued

The Museum has three permanent galleries, one changing exhibit gallery, a children's discovery area, a Heritage Garden, a research and genealogy library, and a gift shop. Special programs for all ages include our Mystery History Tours, Explore Colorado! camps for kids, Focus on Preservation workshops, and our Garden Luncheon. You can visit the Museum Monday through Saturday 10:00am - 4:30pm year round. Call for special summer hours, exhibits, and programs for all ages. Exhibits change three times per year.

Clear Creek History Park

1020 11th Street
Golden, CO 80401
Mailing: 822 12th Street,
Golden, CO 80401
303.278.3557
www.clearcreekhistorypark.org

The Clear Creek History Park is a 3.5 acre "hands-on" educational site in historic downtown Golden, Colorado. The Park interprets the history of the Golden area from 1843-1900. It is founded on a belief that visitors should participate in "hands-on history," and encourages the experiencing, touching, and use of reproduction artifacts. The Park houses a variety of livestock and is in the process of adding greater diversity to the historic breeds on site. Heirloom gardens add a unique dimension to the interpretation of 19th century Colorado.

Spaghetti Sauce

Use this great sauce to top spaghetti, or in lasagna or pizza recipe.

1½ tsp. olive oil
2 cloves garlic, minced
½ onion, chopped (optional)
2 large (28 oz.) cans tomato sauce
1 – 10 oz. can tomato paste
salt and pepper to taste
½ tbsp. each desired (parsley flakes, oregano, Italian seasoning, and marjoram are a nice mix)

Sauté garlic and onion in olive oil. Stir in tomato sauce and tomato paste. Add spices and simmer for about one hour.

Substitute savory for the marjoram if you want a sweeter sauce.

Veggie Tacos

12 taco shells
1 tbsp. olive oil
1 small eggplant (1 lb.),
    peeled and cubed
1 large red bell pepper, chopped
1 small onion, chopped
2 cloves garlic, minced
3 tbsp. salsa or hot sauce
¼ tsp. salt
1/8 tsp. black pepper
low-fat sour cream, salsa, lettuce, grated cheese of your choice

    Warm taco shells in oven as directed on package. Heat oil in skillet over high heat. Add vegetables and garlic. Sauté for 5 minutes or until they begin to brown. Cover. Remove from heat. Let stand 5 minutes or until vegetables begin to soften. Stir in salsa, salt and pepper. Fill warm shells with mixture, top with sour cream, salsa, lettuce, and cheese to taste. Serves 6.

    This recipe can be adapted for the grill. Chop vegetables but not garlic; drizzle with olive oil. Grill over medium-high heat in a "wok" basket for the grill. Grill until veggies begin to brown. Remove from heat and place in heat-proof bowl. Cover. Mince garlic and return to bowl. Let veggies soften slightly. Mix in sour cream, salt and pepper. Serve.

Clear Creek History Park

Continued

    The Park is open for walk-up visitors from May through October, and for scheduled group tours year round. Park construction will end with the construction of a permanent Education and Event Center, slated for 2005. Year round offerings include field trips, special events, such as the Halloween Harvest Festival and Trades, Arts, and Crafts Festival, evening programs, volunteer programs, partnerships with other cultural institutions, and a children's summer program.

Garbanzo Beans & Rice

1 tbsp. olive oil
2 cups onion, sliced
½ tsp. cumin seed (not ground)
1 cup red bell pepper, sliced
1 tbsp. water
½ cup green onion, sliced

¼ tsp. salt
2 15 oz. cans garbanzo beans, drained
2 cups fresh basil, chopped
¼ cup garlic & herb bread crumbs
2 cups cooked brown rice

Heat oil in large skillet. Add onion and cumin seed. Sauté 10 minutes or until onion is lightly browned. Add bell pepper and water; reduce heat, cover, and simmer 3 minutes. Add green onions, salt, and garbanzos. Cover and cook 2 minutes or until thoroughly heated, stirring occasionally. Remove from heat; stir in basil. Sprinkle with bread crumbs. Serve over rice.

Southwestern Risotto

1¾ cups water
2 14 oz. cans vegetable broth
2 tsp. olive oil
1 cup uncooked Arborio rice
1 tsp. ground cumin
1 tsp. ground coriander
4 cloves garlic, minced

1 cup green onions, diced
¾ cup Monterey Jack with jalapeno cheese,
    shredded
½ tsp. Frank's Red Hot sauce
2 cups frozen kernel corn
¾ cup roasted red bell pepper, chopped*

*You may use bottled red peppers, but for a fresher flavor, roast whole peppers under the broiler or on a grill until the skins blister and "pop", then peel, seed, and chop.

In a medium saucepan combine water and broth. Bring to simmer. Keep warm on low. Heat oil in a large skillet over medium-high heat. Add rice, cumin, coriander and garlic. Sauté 1 minute. Stir in ½ cup broth and cook until liquid is nearly absorbed, stirring constantly. In small amounts, add remaining broth and stir. Process should take about 20 minutes. Stir in onion, cheese, Red Hot sauce, corn and peppers. Cook until thoroughly heated, about 4 minutes.

Salsa Tempeh Couscous

2 packages couscous
1 tbsp. olive oil
1/4 cup chopped almonds
4 garlic cloves, minced
8 oz. tempeh (mixed grain)
2 cups salsa

½ cup water
4 tbsp. dried currants
2 tbsp. honey
1 ½ tsp. cumin
1 tsp. cinnamon

In a bowl combine salsa, water, currants, honey, garlic, cumin, and cinnamon. Cut tempeh into 1" cubes, place in salsa mixture and toss to gently coat all sides. Let stand for 10 minutes. In medium skillet over medium-high heat toast almonds in oil until golden, 3-4 minutes. Set aside. Remove tempeh with a slotted spoon and place in skillet. Cook until all sides are browned (5-8 min). Add salsa mixture and cook until hot. Prepare couscous according to package directions. Serve salsa mixture over couscous. Top with almonds. Serves 4.

Drunken Beans

12 ounces dry pinto beans
1 onion, chopped
2 garlic cloves, crushed
1 tbsp. oil
1 cup Coors or Killian's Irish Red beer
1 cup canned chopped tomatoes

1 jalapeño, seeded, chopped
1 tsp. salt
1 tsp. sugar
1/2 tsp. pepper
1/2 cup cilantro, chopped

Soak beans, covered with water, overnight in a large bowl. Drain.

Place the pinto beans in a large pot and cover with 1" water. Bring to a boil; reduce the heat and cook covered about 1/2 hour. In a skillet over high heat, sauté chopped onion and crushed garlic cloves in oil until tender, about 10 minutes. Add to the beans along with beer, tomatoes, jalapeno, salt, sugar, and pepper. Simmer, covered another 30 minutes. Remove from the heat and stir in chopped cilantro.

Artichoke Melanise

2 pkg. frozen artichoke hearts, thawed
   or 2 14 oz. cans artichoke hearts,
    drained
½ cup butter
2 cups sliced fresh mushrooms
1 tsp. salt
1 tsp. sweet basil, crushed
½ tsp. oregano, crushed
¼ tsp. garlic powder
1 tbsp. fine dry bread crumbs
2 tbsp. lemon juice
½ cup parmesan cheese

    Melt butter in large heavy pan. Sauté mushrooms until golden. Sprinkle with salt and rest of dry ingredients during cooking. Stir in. When mushrooms are golden, stir in bread crumbs and lemon juice, mixing well.

    Arrange artichoke hearts in a lightly buttered shallow glass baking dish. Spoon mushroom mix over all. Sprinkle with cheese and bake in 350 degree oven 25 – 30 minutes, until juice bubbles and cheese is browned. Serves 6 – 8.

Asparagus with Prosciutto

Prosciutto adds a wonderful rich and salty taste to any vegetable it is paired with. You can find it with the specialty meats at almost any supermarket.

2 pounds asparagus, trimmed
¼ cup butter
3 ounces thinly sliced prosciutto, chopped
2 cloves garlic, minced
½ cup pine nuts (pinon)
1/3 cup lemon juice
salt
pepper to taste

In a large saucepan bring to boil enough lightly salted water to cover asparagus. Add asparagus. Cook 3 minutes or until tender-crisp; drain. Place asparagus into bowl of iced water. Let stand until cool but not cold; drain. Arrange on serving platter.

While asparagus is cooling, melt butter in large skillet. Over medium heat sauté the prosciutto, garlic, and pine nuts for 2 minutes. Stir in lemon juice. Season to taste with salt and pepper. Pour over asparagus.

Baked Corn

1 15 oz. can cream style corn	½ cup cracker crumbs
½ tsp. salt	1 cup milk
1 tsp. sugar	butter
3 eggs	ground black pepper

Preheat oven to 375°. Stir salt and sugar into creamed corn. Beat in eggs. Add cracker crumbs and milk and mix thoroughly. Pour into baking dish. Dot with butter and pepper. Bake 45 minutes to 1 hour.

German Spaetzle Noodles

Ida Goetze, the German widow who ran the Astor House as a boarding house from the 1890's until the 1950's, might have prepared a meal like this in her kitchen. Spaetzle is a very popular German comfort food and is often served with Schnitzel (breaded veal cutlets) or venison.

13 oz. flour	1 tbsp. oil
2 eggs	pinch salt
½ pint water	

Mix the flour, eggs and salt to form a dough; add the water until the dough is smooth and not too thick (depending on the size of the eggs, possibly slightly less than ½ pint).

Knead the dough (e.g. with the dough hook of a mixer) until air bubbles appear. The dough should be stretchy (not like a cookie dough). Heat a large pan of salted water and add 1 tbsp. oil Fill a Spaetzle form with some of the dough and press the dough through into the boiling water; or, if you do not have a form, stretch the dough onto a wet cutting board and use a knife (dipped in hot water) to scrape small lumps of dough into the boiling water (like gnocchi, only much smaller).

When the noodles float to the surface, remove with a slotted spoon and keep warm. Repeat this process until all the dough has been cooked. Serve Spaetlze topped with browned butter and chopped fresh parsley. For variety, you can melt some grated cheese into the noodles. Serves 4 people.

Rice Supreme

1 ½ cups uncooked rice
1 stick butter
2 cans mushroom soup
1 medium jar (13 oz.) mushrooms with liquid
5 green onions
10 oz. grated cheddar cheese
toasted sliced almonds

Cook the rice. Melt butter and sauté onions. Add the mushroom soup and mushrooms in the butter and pour over rice. Mix. Pour into a 12" x 8" x 2". Top with cheese and almonds. Bake at 350° for 15 minutes. Serves 12.

Wild Rice Stuffed Squash

2 acorn or butternut squash, halved and seeded
salt and pepper
2 cups cooked wild rice (about ½ cup uncooked)
½ tsp. seasoned salt
2 tsp. grated orange rind
1 tbsp. brown sugar
1 cup chopped nuts (pecans, if possible)
apricot or orange juice, about ½ cup
2 tsp. brown sugar, optional

Preheat oven to 350°. Salt and pepper the squash cavities to taste. Fill the cavities with a mixture of the wild rice, seasoned salt, orange rind, brown sugar and chopped nuts. Bake, covered, for 1 hour (or longer if cooking more or larger squash), basting occasionally with the fruit juice. When squash is tender, sprinkle ½ teaspoon brown sugar atop each squash, if desired, and serve. Serves 4 generously.

Hawaiian Style Parsnips

2 pounds parsnips (10 medium)
2 tbsp. brown sugar
1 tbsp. corn starch
¾ tsp. salt
1 8¼ oz. can crushed pineapple
½ tsp. finely shredded orange peel
½ cup orange juice
2 tbsp. butter or margarine

Peel and slice parsnips. If using larger parsnips, be sure to core them. Cook covered in a small amount of boiling salted water until tender (15 – 20 minutes). In a large saucepan, combine brown sugar, cornstarch, and ¾ tsp. salt; stir in undrained pineapple, orange peel and orange juice. Cook and stir until thickened and bubbly. Cook and stir 2 minutes more. Add butter, stir until melted. Add parsnips. Cover and heat through, about 5 minutes. Crisp fried and crumbled bacon makes an excellent topping for this dish. Serves 6 – 8.

Snowy Mashed Potato Casserole

12 medium Russet potatoes
   (approx. 4 lbs.)
8 oz. package cream cheese, softened
1 cup dairy sour cream
1/8 tsp. pepper
1 tsp. salt
1 clove garlic, chopped finely
    (or equivalent in garlic powder)
¼ cup chopped chives
small amount of milk
½ tsp. paprika
1 tbsp. butter

Preheat oven to 350º. Cook potatoes, mash them partly and then put in mixer to thoroughly soften them. Add cream cheese, sour cream, pepper, salt, and garlic. Beat until smooth, and then stir in chopped chives. If the mixture is pretty stiff, add a little milk to soften it. Put in a greased deep baking dish. Put butter and paprika on top. Bake for 40 – 45 minutes until heated through and golden on the top. This can be prepared a day ahead and refrigerated, then baked on the day it is to be served.

Freezer Potatoes

10 large potatoes
1 8 oz. package cream cheese, softened
1 cup milk
½ cup butter, softened

Peel, boil, and mash potatoes. Mix the remainder of the ingredients and add to the warm mashed potatoes. Turn into a greased casserole dish and freeze. When ready to use, thaw and bake 1 1/2 hours at 375º or until brown.

Sweet Potatoes Caribbean Style

This recipe is a wonderful variation on the traditional holiday sweet potato side dish. It is terrific with grilled chicken or turkey. Plantains are found in the produce section with the exotic fruits. They are fully ripe when the skins turn completely black and yield under slight pressure.

7 cups sweet potato, peeled and cubed
2 cups very ripe plantain, peeled and sliced
1/3 cup light brown sugar
¼ cup fat free milk
¼ cup light sour cream
¼ tsp. ground allspice
cooking spray
¼ cup pitted dates, chopped
¼ cup slivered almonds, toasted

Preheat over to 350º. Spray 1½ quart baking dish with cooking spray, set aside. Place potato in a large saucepan, cover with water; bring to a boil. Reduce heat; simmer 7 minutes or until slightly soft. Add plantain, simmer 7 more minutes or until very tender. Drain. Return potato and plantain to pan, add milk, sugar, sour cream, and allspice. With mixer, beat 2 minutes at high speed until smooth. Transfer to prepared baking dish. Sprinkle with dates and almonds. Bake 30 minutes or until thoroughly heated. Serves 6.

Sweet Potato Casserole

3 lbs sweet potatoes
½ cup sugar
2 eggs
1 tsp. vanilla
½ cup milk
½ cup butter, softened

Topping:
1/3 cup flour
1/3 cup butter, softened
1 cup brown sugar
1 cup pecans, chopped

Boil the sweet potatoes for about 45 minutes, or until cooked through. Let sweet potatoes cool, remove the skins. Mash thoroughly. Preheat oven to 350º. Mix together sugar, eggs, vanilla, milk, and butter and pour into a greased 9" x 13" pan.

Mix together the topping ingredients with a pastry knife. Spread topping on the mashed sweet potato mixture. Bake for 30 minutes or until hot and bubbly. Serves 8.

Cranberry Relish

This colorful recipe is fast becoming a staple at our Christmas teas. Don't hesitate to serve it as a salad. There is no need to partner it with a main dish as a relish.

1 bag fresh cranberries, coarsely ground
1 cup pecan pieces
1 small can crushed pineapple, drained
2 medium apples, diced
1 small can mandarin oranges, drained
1 cup sugar

Mix all ingredients. Chill and serve.

Oven Apple Butter

2 quarts water   3½ to 4 cups sugar
2 tbsp. salt   1 tsp. cinnamon
6 pounds apples, peeled and sliced   ½ tsp. ground cloves
2 quarts sweet cider   ½ tsp. allspice

Combine water and salt. Add apples. Drain well but do not rinse slices. Grind through the finest blade of a food mill. Measure pulp and juices (should be about 2 quarts). Combine with cider. Place in large enamel pan. Center pan in moderate over, about 350°. Let mixture simmer until cooked down about half and is thick and mushy, about 3 to 3 ½ hours, stirring every half hour. Put mixture through sieve or food mill; should yield about 2 ¼ to 2½ quarts. Combine sugar and spices; add to sauce and return mixture to oven. Continue simmering about 1½ hours or until thick, stirring every half hour. To test, pour small amount onto cold plate. If no liquid oozes around edge then the apple butter is ready.

Pour into hot, sterilized jars and seal. Makes 2 quarts.

Sweet & Sour Mustard

1 cup dry mustard
1 cup white vinegar
1 cup sugar
1 tbsp. salt
2 large eggs, beaten

Mix dry mustard and vinegar and let stand overnight. Add remaining ingredients and cook until thick in a double boiler. Seal and store in the refrigerator.

Kraut Relish

1 12-oz can sauerkraut, well drained
1 cup chopped green pepper
1 cup chopped celery
1 cup chopped onion
1 2-oz can chopped pimento (optional)
½ cup sugar
½ cup vinegar

In a covered saucepan, heat and blend sugar and vinegar. This becomes the marinade for the other ingredients. Refrigerate combined ingredients and marinate overnight. Keeps for weeks in the refrigerator. Good with any meat dish.

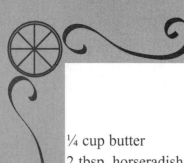

Horseradish Sauce

¼ cup butter
2 tbsp. horseradish
1 tbsp. very thick cream
½ tsp. apple cider vinegar

Cream butter till very light. Add two tablespoonfuls of grated, cooked and cooled horseradish, one tablespoonful of very thick cream, and half a teaspoonful of apple cider vinegar.

This recipe was prepared at our 2002 Halloween Harvest Festival, using fresh horseradish grown in the History Park's heirloom garden.

Hot Relish

4 quarts ripe tomatoes (or canned)
1 pound hot peppers, ground
2 large onions
2 tbsp. chili powder
2 tbsp. salt
2 cups sugar
2 cups vinegar
5 cloves garlic

Cook to desired consistency and seal while hot; 45 minutes or more.
Yields 7 - 9 pints

A Fine Finish

Colorado is a great bicycling state. As early as 1883, Golden had a bicycle club. Famous families in Golden's history, such as West and Parfet, appear in cycling news reports of the time. In addition, cyclists from the many Denver cycling clubs often rode west to Golden, and then climbed the Mount Vernon canyon road as well as Chimney Gulch trail to get into the mountains. A "rail trail," smooth crushed stone between the rails, was established from Golden through Clear Creek Canyon to Central City and Black Hawk. Another rail trail came into Golden from the east along the north side of Clear Creek. A century later, in the 1980s, the area was made famous for cycling again with the Red Zinger and Coors' Classic races starting and ending in Golden. These are immortalized in the movie "The American Flyer," shot in the Golden area.

(Photo: Sara Bicknell, Golden resident and cyclist, c.1896; courtesy of the Golden Pioneer Museum)

Cranberry Ice

A great alternative to jellied cranberries during the holidays! This can be made in an ice cream freezer.

4 cups fresh cranberries
4 cups water
2 cups sugar
¼ cup lemon juice

Place cranberries and 2 cups water in large saucepan. Cook over medium heat until the skin is broken on the cranberries. Drain. Using a food mill or strainer, strain the cranberries to pulp into a large mixing bowl. Discard skins. Add remaining 2 cups water, sugar, and lemon juice to cranberry pulp. Mix thoroughly. Put bowl of cranberry mixture in freezer. Whip each ¼ hour until frozen, will be fairly thick. Using an ice cream scoop or large spoon, put frozen cranberry mixture into single-serve dishes. Place bowls back in freezer until ready to serve. Serve from freezer to table. Serves 8 - 10.

Apple or Pear Kuchen

½ cup butter, softened
1 package yellow cake mix
½ cup flaked coconut
1 cup canned, sliced apples
   or 2 ½ cups fresh baking apples, or
1 cup canned, sliced pears

   or 2 ½ cups fresh pears
1/2 cup sugar
1 cup dairy sour cream
1 tsp. cinnamon
2 egg yolks or 1 whole egg

Preheat over to 350º. Cut butter into cake mix until crumbly. Mix in coconut. Pat mixture lightly into ungreased 13 x 9 x 2 pan building edges up slightly. Bake 10 minutes. Arrange apple slices or pear slices on warm crust. Mix sugar and cinnamon and sprinkle over apples. Blend sour cream and egg; drizzle over apples. Bake 25 minutes or until edges are light brown. Serve warm if you wish. Serves 12 - 15.

Rhubarb Custard Kuchen

1 cup flour
½ cup margarine
½ cup powdered sugar
1 ½ cup sugar
¼ tsp. nutmeg
¾ tsp. baking powder
2 eggs
2 cups raw, finely chopped rhubarb

Cut margarine into flour and powdered sugar. Press into 8" x 12" pan. Bake 15 minutes at 350º. Watch carefully as it browns easily. Beat together sugar, nutmeg, baking powder, and eggs. Add rhubarb and stir. Spread on hot dough. Return to oven. Bake at 350° for 40 - 50 minutes.

Rice Pudding

1 quart milk
1 cup sugar
1 cup rice (use basmati or Jasmin rice)
8 cardamom pods
1 inch piece of cinnamon
pinch of saffron or tumeric
½ cup raisins or currants

Combine first six ingredients and cook barely simmering in uncovered pot for 45 minutes. Stir every few minutes to incorporate skin forming on top. After 45 minutes, remove cinnamon stick and cardamom pods. Add raisins and simmer another 5 minutes. Let cool. Serve at room temperature or refrigerated.

Golden Oldy Cyclery

303.271.1998
www.brekus.org/wheelmen/
goldenoldy

Golden Oldy Cyclery is a private cycling museum open to the public by appointment and at special Open Houses announced in the Golden Transcript newspaper. It has a theme of Victorian Cycling and specializes on the 1880 to 1899 period. A hallmark of the period was the High Wheel "Penny Farthing" bicycle. Golden Oldy Cyclery focuses on this style and carries 3 prominent brands of "pennies": Columbia, Victor, and Rudge.

Strawberry Sublime

Crust:
1 cup flour
¼ cup brown sugar
½ cup butter
½ cup walnuts

Filling:
1 cup sugar
2 tbsp. lemon juice
2 egg whites
10 oz. frozen strawberries - partly thawed
½ pint whipping cream
½ tsp. vanilla

Crust:
Preheat oven to 350°. Mix together crust ingredients until they form crumbles. Bake 10 minutes on a cookie sheet, stirring twice.

Filling:
Beat first 4 filling ingredients for 15 minutes. Fold in beaten whipping cream and vanilla. Sprinkle ½ of the cooked crumb mix in a 9" x 13" pan. Cover with the filling. Sprinkle with the other half of crumbs. Cover and freeze at least 6 hours. Slice and serve.

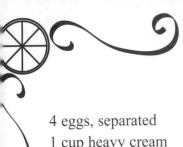

Fruit Torte

4 eggs, separated
1 cup heavy cream
1 tsp. vanilla extract
1 cup sugar
1 pint strawberries or fresh
   peaches
liqueur if desired
½ cup shortening (margarine),
   softened

½ cup sugar
1 cup flour
1 tsp. baking powder
½ tsp. salt
5 tbsp. milk
Cointreau or Grand Marnier

Slice fruit into big chunks and marinate in Cointreau or Grand Marnier. Refrigerate while assembling torte. Whip cream until peaks form. Add vanilla extract and refrigerate.

Preheat oven to 325°. Grease and carefully flour two 12" pizza pans. Cream together shortening and ½ cup sugar. Beat in egg yolks. Combine flour, baking powder and salt. Add to mixture alternately with milk. Mix very well. Spread half of cake dough carefully on each pizza pan, going as evenly as possible to the edges. Carefully spread half the whipped cream on top of each cake layer. Bake for about 15 - 25 minutes, until meringue is golden brown. Cool 15 minutes.

Place one layer on large cake dish, meringue side down; cover with whipped cream and fruit, evenly arranged. Place second layer, meringue side up, on the fruit. Refrigerate several hours before serving, to allow flavors to blend. Serves 10 - 12 generously; can be cut into small slices for about 24 people.

Golden Oldy Cyclery

Continued

The museum's main room is laid out as a bicycle shop from 1889, complete with all of the cycling accessories and shop fixtures for that period. Wall décor includes period advertising posters and Victorian period photos. Other rooms display specialty bikes, cycling headware, and clothing of the late Victorian period. The Colorado Cycling Photo Gallery features copies of vintage photos all taken in Colorado. The museum also contains a reference library with 30,000 microfilm pages, 400 bound volumes, and 200 journals.

Popcorn Crunch

2 quarts popped corn
1 1/3 cups sugar
1 cup margarine
½ cup Karo clear syrup
1 tsp. vanilla

Combine sugar, margarine, and Karo syrup in a heavy saucepan. Bring to a boil over medium heat, stirring occasionally. Cook to 270° (soft crack stage), then remove from heat. Working quickly, stir in vanilla and pour mixture over popcorn and mix thoroughly. Spread out on waxed paper and break apart.

Peanut Butter Candy

Kids love this treat! It is easy enough for them to make, besides being nutritious. The rolls can be coated with chopped dates or grated coconut for extra goodness.

1 cup creamy peanut butter
1 cup honey
2 cups instant dry milk
¼ cup wheat germ
¼ cup raisins

In a medium bowl mix peanut butter and honey together with a spoon. Add dry milk and wheat germ. Mix using the spoon to start, but it will take your hands to finish kneading until smooth. Add raisins and continue to knead until they are spread through mixture. Divide in half and make two rolls about 1½" in diameter. Wrap rolls in wax paper and place in refrigerator. When cold, unwrap one end and slice in ½ inch pieces, only as many as needed at one time. Keep refrigerated, as the cold rolls are easier to slice.

Cherry One-Bowl Cake

2 cups flour
1 cup sugar
2 tsp. baking soda
1 tsp. salt
½ tsp. cinnamon
½ tsp. nutmeg
1 can cherry pie filling
2 eggs
½ cup salad oil
1 tsp. vanilla
½ cup sliced almonds
powdered sugar to taste

Preheat oven to 325°. Sift dry ingredients together. Lightly stir in all other ingredients except powdered sugar, putting nuts in last. Oil a 9" x 13" pan. Pour batter into pan. Bake one hour. Let cool in pan. Sift the powdered sugar over top.

Variation: Use apple pie filling; replace almonds with 1 cup walnuts, and omit nutmeg.

Torture Cake

This is called Torture Cake because the family sees the cake every time they look in the refrigerator for three days and then the cook takes the cake to serve at a party!

Cake:
1 box German chocolate cake mix
1 ¼ cups water
1/3 cup oil
3 eggs

Make cake according to boxed direction in two 9" layer pans. Cool completely then cut each layer horizontally to fill.*

Filling:
1 16 oz. carton sour cream
2 cups sugar
1 tsp. vanilla
5 ounces flaked coconut

Mix ingredients together and spread over bottom layer of each layer cake. Place top layer of each layer cake over filling.

Icing:
1 16 oz. carton frozen whipped topping, thawed
5 ounces flaked coconut
1 tsp. vanilla

Mix whipped topping and vanilla together; spread over top and sides of cakes. Sprinkle with coconut.

Refrigerate cakes 2 to 3 days before serving.

*An easy way to split the cake layers is to line up dental floss halfway around the side of the layer, cross the ends of the floss and pull tightly until the layer is cut through.

Trés Leches Cake
(3 Milks Cake)

A fabulous dessert from Central America. It's a bit labor intensive, but worth every minute of it. This is a lighter version.

Cake:

Canola cooking spray
2/3 cup plus 1 tbsp. flour
¼ tsp. salt

4 egg whites
2/3 cup sugar
1 tsp. vanilla
3 large eggs

Preheat oven to 350°. Coat a 13" x 9" baking pan with cooking spray and dust with 1 tbsp. flour. Beat together salt and egg whites in large mixer bowl until soft peaks form. Add sugar, a little at a time; beat until stiff peaks form. In a separate bowl, beat together vanilla and eggs until thick and pale yellow (3 minutes). Gently fold egg whites into egg mixture. Gradually add flour. Pour into prepared pan. Bake 20 minutes or until top springs back when lightly touched (do not stick a toothpick in it!). Cool 5 minutes on wire rack.

Milks:

1 cup half-and-half
1 14 ounce can fat free sweetened condensed milk
1 12 ounce can fat free evaporated milk

Combine all in a bowl. Pierce top of cake with a fork and pour milk mixture over the top.

Meringue:

3 egg whites
1 cup sugar

1/3 cup water
1 tsp. lemon rind, minced
1 tsp. vanilla

Beat together egg whites until foamy. In a saucepan, combine sugar and water; bring to boil. Cook without stirring until a candy thermometer reads 238°. Pour syrup into egg whites, beating at high speed. Stir in lemon rind and vanilla. Spread over cake.

Terrific if served at room temperature with sliced strawberries.

Blackberry and Apple Pudding

3 cooking apples
2 cups berries (blackberries, raspberries, or
    strawberries)
½ cup sugar
½ tsp. cinnamon
6 tbsp. butter, softened
2 eggs, lightly beaten

1 cup flour
2 tbsp. cornstarch
2 tbsp. powdered sugar
1 cup whipping cream
1 tbsp. sugar
1 tsp. vanilla

Preheat oven to 375°. Peel, core, and slice the apples thinly. Combine apples with the berries. Add ¼ cup of the sugar and cinnamon, and place in a buttered 1 ½ quart baking dish. Beat together the remaining sugar and butter until fluffy. Beat in the eggs. Sift the flour with the cornstarch and add to the butter mixture. Spread over the fruit and bake for 40 minutes. Dust the top of the pudding with sifted powdered sugar and serve hot with whipped cream.

Whipped cream: Pour the cream into a bowl and whip until thickened slightly. Add 1 tbsp. sugar and continue beating until thick. Add 1 tsp. of vanilla extract. Serves 6.

Aunt Betty's Banana Pudding

This is from my book group; we only circulate recipes when they are really good!

2 (3.4 oz.) packages instant vanilla pudding
    mix
1 cup milk
1 (14 oz.) can sweetened condensed milk
1 (8 oz.) container sour cream

1 (8 oz.) container frozen whipped topping,
    thawed
6 bananas, sliced
½ (12 oz.) package vanilla wafers

In a medium bowl, combine pudding mix and milk and stir until mix is dissolved. Refrigerate 15 minutes until partially set. Stir condensed milk into pudding mixture until smooth. Fold in sour cream and whipped topping. Fold in bananas. Make a single layer of vanilla wafers in the bottom of a 9" x 13" dish. Spread pudding evenly over wafers. Crush remaining wafers and sprinkle on top. Refrigerate until serving. Serves 10.

Windows on the World Amaretto Soufflé

Windows on the World was located on the 107th floor of the World Trade Center in New York. I had enjoyed this light dessert on my visits there.

4 macaroon cookies

6 egg yolks

2 eggs

¾ cup sugar

¼ cup Amaretto liquor

2 cups whipping cream, whipped

additional whipping cream

   and macaroons for topping

   Crumble macaroons into small pieces. Spread into shallow baking dish and dry at 300° for 20 minutes, stirring once. Cool. In a large bowl combine egg yolks, whole eggs, and sugar. Beat on high until thick and fluffy and sugar is dissolved, about 5 minutes. Continue beating and gradually add liquor. Gently fold in whipped cream and ¾ cup macaroon crumbs. Prepare six 6-ounce ramekins with buttered 1-inch aluminum foil "collars" or a 1.5 quart soufflé with a buttered 2.5 inch collar. Gently spoon mixture into dishes and freeze 4 - 6 hours. To serve, top with additional whipped cream and macaroon crumbs.

Chocolate Mousse Pie

1 cup milk chocolate chips

½ cup milk

2 tbsp. powdered sugar

3-ounces cream cheese, softened

8-ounces Cool Whip

1 8" chocolate pie crust

   Melt chocolate chips in 2 tablespoons milk. Beat sugar into the softened cream cheese. Add remaining milk and chocolate mixture to the cream cheese. Fold in Cool Whip and spoon into crust. Freeze until firm, about 24 hours.

Honey Quiche

1 can sweetened condensed milk
1 cup milk
½ cup honey
1/8 tsp. saffron
1 cup heavy cream
3 eggs
2 8" unbaked pie shells

Preheat oven to 350°. Over medium heat, combine milk, cream and saffron but do not boil. Beat eggs and honey together, warm over low heat. Combine milk mixture with egg mixture, ½ cup at a time. Pour into pie shells. Bake approximately 30 to 40 minutes until set and light gold in color. Chill. Garnish with nutmeg. Makes two 8" pies.

Anise Biscotti

4 eggs
¾ cup sugar
½ cup shortening
¼ bottle of anise flavoring
1 ½ tbsp. baking powder
3 cups flour

Cream together shortening and sugar. Add eggs and anise. Add flour and baking powder. Form into 4 loaves. Bake in a 350° oven until brown on top (20 - 30 minutes) Slice into ½ inch slices and lay them down on a cookie sheet and bake them again until they are crunchy and lightly browned.

Easy Stained Glass Window Cookies

Very festive for holidays like Valentine's Day, Easter, and Christmas.

1 roll refrigerated sugar cookie dough, divided
      or 1 batch of your favorite sugar cookie recipe
¼ cup flour, sifted
¾ cup finely crushed translucent hard candy, such as Jolly Ranchers *

Line cookie sheet with parchment paper or foil. Preheat oven to 350º. Sprinkle flour into a non-stick surface. Roll out ½ of cookie dough to about ¼" thickness. Cut into shapes with 2" or larger cookie cutters. Place on baking sheet about 2" apart. Cut smaller shape into center of each cookie, leaving at least ¼" of cookie dough on each edge. Fill cutout centers with enough candy to fill the hole when melted. Bake for 7-8 minutes or until slightly golden. Cool on sheets for 1 minute, then slide foil with cookies off onto a wire rack to cool completely. Repeat with remaining dough.

    * If using more than 1 color or flavor of candy, keep the flavors/colors separated; otherwise they will taste and look odd.

Golden Public Library

Continued
In fifty years, the library system has grown to be recognized as one of the top 25 most technologically progressive library systems in the nation. From patron surveys, JCPL ranked one of the most service-oriented organizations in the state. A quality public library is key to building a strong community. Cooperation with other organizations such as the City and the Golden Cultural Alliance is part of our mission.

Lemon Angel Pie

4 eggs, room temperature, separated
2¾ cups sugar, divided
½ tsp. cream of tartar
1½ cups whipping cream
  or 8 to 12 oz. of Cool Whip
4 tbsp. cornstarch

4 tbsp. flour
dash salt
2 cups hot water
1 tsp. grated fresh lemon peel
2 2/3 tbsp. butter or margarine
½ cup fresh lemon juice

For meringue: grease 9" x 13" pan. Preheat oven to 275°. Beat egg whites in medium bowl until foamy. Add cream of tartar and beat until glossy. Add one cup of sugar, a little at a time, beating constantly. Beat until stiff and all sugar is disolved. Spread evenly in pan. Bake at 275° for 20 minutes; then bake at 300° for 40 minutes. Turn off oven; leave in oven for 2 hours.

For middle layer: Whip cream. Spread carefully on top of cooled meringue. If using Cool Whip, substitute this for the whipped cream. Refrigerate dish while preparing topping.

For topping: In saucepan mix 1¾ cups sugar, cornstarch, flour, and salt. Gradually blend in hot water. Bring to boiling over high heat, stirring constantly. Reduce heat to medium; cook and stir 8 minutes more. Do not allow to burn, reduce heat if necessary. Remove from heat.

Beat egg yolks slightly. Stir small amount hot mixture into egg yolks; then return all to hot mixture. Bring to a boil over high heat, stirring constantly. Reduce heat to low; cook and stir 4 minutes longer. Remove from heat. Add lemon peel and butter. Gradually stir in lemon juice. Cover pot with clear plastic wrap; cool 10 minutes. Uncover and cool to room temperature. Place lemon mixture carefully on top of whipped cream layer. If you start in the corners and put little dots of lemon everywhere, then spread the, it generally works better than spooning it all in the middle and trying to spread it out. Chill until serving. Cut into bars to serve. Serves 9.

Old Fashioned Custard Pie

2 ½ cups scalded milk
½ cup sugar
3 eggs
1/3 tsp. salt
1 tsp. vanilla
9" deep dish unbaked pie shell
nutmeg to sprinkle on top

Add sugar to scalded milk. Stir until dissolved. Beat eggs with salt, slightly. Gradually add milk, then vanilla. Stir. Pour into pie shell. Sprinkle top with nutmeg. Bake at 400° for 10 minutes, then turn oven down to 350° and bake for 25 minutes, or until knife is clean, when custard has set.

Jewish Apple Cake

3 cups flour, sifted
2 cups sugar + 2 tbsp.
1 cup oil
3 tsp. baking powder
4 eggs
¼ cup orange juice
2 ½ tsp. vanilla
3 or 4 apples, peeled and sliced
2 tsp cinnamon

Preheat oven to 375°. Liberally grease a large tube pan. Beat together flour, 2 cups sugar, oil, baking powder, eggs, and orange juice until smooth. Mix cinnamon and 2 tablespoons sugar, sprinkle tube pan with half of mixture. Layer in half of apples, batter, cinnamon and sugar mix, then repeat layers. Bake for 1¼ to 1½ hours.

Oatmeal Chocolate Chip Cake

1 ¾ cups flour
1 tsp. baking soda
½ tsp. salt
1 tbsp. cocoa
1¾ cups boiling water
1 cup uncooked oatmeal
½ cup white sugar

1 cup light brown sugar, packed
½ cup butter, softened
2 large eggs, slightly beaten
1 12 oz. package semi-sweet chocolate
    chips
chopped walnuts, if desired

Preheat oven to 350°. Combine flour, soda, salt, and cocoa. Set aside. In a large bowl, pour boiling water over oatmeal; let stand for ten minutes. Add sugars and butter, stir until butter is melted. Add eggs and mix with a spoon. Add flour mixture and ½ package of chocolate chips. Pour batter into a greased 9" x 13" pan. Sprinkle nuts (if desired) and remaining chocolate chips on top. Bake 40 minutes.

Sour Cherry Cake

¼ cup shortening
¾ cup sugar
1 egg
1 ½ cup sifted flour
2 tsp. baking powder
½ tsp. salt
½ cup milk
1 can (1 lb.) tart red pitted cherries, drained
½ tsp. almond extract

Preheat oven to 350°. Grease an 8"x8"x2" pan. Cream together shortening and sugar. Add egg and beat well. In a separate bowl, sift together flour, baking powder and salt. Add to egg mixture alternately with milk. Stir just to blend. Fold in cherries and almond extract. Turn into pan. Bake for 50 minutes or until a toothpick inserted in the center comes out clean.

Tiramisu

This decadent Italian specialty is very labor intensive, but definitely worth the effort for the chocolate and coffee lover.

24 lady fingers,
   or 2 - 8" x 8" sponge cakes
5 large egg yolks
1/3 cup + 2 tbsp. sugar
1/3 cup Marsala
1 tbsp. water
½ cup heavy cream

2 tsp. vanilla
12 ounces mascarpone cheese, softened
1 cup espresso (or strong coffee), cooled
2 tbsp. rum, brandy or amaretto
5 ounces bittersweet chocolate, grated
1 tbsp. unsweetened cocoa powder

Preheat oven to 350°. If using sponge cake, cut one and a half into strips. Cut strips in half. Arrange lady fingers or cake slices on a baking sheet. Bake until golden brown and crisp, about 8 - 10 minutes. Cool.

Meanwhile, in a medium, heat-proof bowl beat together egg yolks and 1/3 cup sugar until thick and pale yellow, about 2 minutes. Add Marsala and water. Set bowl over a simmering saucepan of water and whisk until mixture reaches 160°. Remove from saucepan and cool for 15 minutes, stirring occasionally. In a separate bowl, beat together heavy cream and vanilla until soft peaks form. Fold in mascarpone cheese and cooled egg mixture. In a small bowl or container with a spout mix together espresso, rum, and 2 tbsp. sugar. Place half of lady fingers in bottom of a flat-bottomed serving dish. Pour half of espresso mixture over lady fingers. Spread with half of mascarpone mixture. Sprinkle with half of bittersweet chocolate. Top with remaining lady fingers, spread with remaining cheese mixture, sprinkle with remaining chocolate. Over the top sift the cocoa powder. Cover with plastic wrap. Chill for at least 1 hour and up to 24 hours before serving. Serves 8 – 10.

Amaretto Tiramisu

For those seeking a lighter, healthier version of Tiramisu, this recipe is just for you!

8 ounces Neufchatel cheese, room temperature
1/3 cup sugar
5 tbsp. amaretto liqueur
½ tsp. vanilla
3 cups reduced fat non-dairy whipped topping
24 lady fingers
¾ cup strong coffee
¼ cup unsweetened cocoa powder
1 tbsp. powdered sugar
2 tbsp. almonds, blanched

Beat together cream cheese and sugar in medium bowl until light and creamy. Add in Amaretto and vanilla. Gradually fold in whipped topping. Arrange lady fingers in bottom of 9" x 9" baking dish. Sprinkle with half of coffee, top with half of the cream cheese mixture. Sprinkle with half of the cocoa powder, repeat layers, ending with cocoa. Cover and refrigerate at least 4 hours, preferably overnight. Sprinkle with powdered sugar and almonds.

Devil's Food Float

½ cup sweet milk
1 tsp. vanilla
2 tbsp. melted margarine
½ cup chopped nuts
1 cup flour
¼ tsp. salt
¾ cup sugar
2 tsp. baking powder

1½ tbsp. cocoa
½ cup chopped walnuts

Topping:
1 cup white sugar
2 tbsp. cocoa
1 cup hot water

Preheat oven to 350°. Grease 9"x9" pan. In a saucepan, melt margarine. Then add milk and vanilla. Sift together all dry ingredients except the nuts and then add to milk mixture. Mix gently, then add nuts. In a saucepan, heat to boiling topping ingredients. Pour hot topping over mixture in pan and bake for 40 minutes. Serve upside down when cool.

Poppyseed Cake

3 cups flour
   for high altitude use 3¼ cups
½ tsp. salt
1½ tsp. baking powder
3 eggs
2¼ cup sugar

1 1/8 cup cooking oil
1½ cup milk
3 tbsp. poppy seeds
1½ tsp. almond extract
1½ tsp. vanilla extract

Preheat oven to 350°. Grease a tube pan. Mix all ingredients. Bake for one hour or until toothpick inserted in center of cake comes out clean. Cool slightly, then with a long skewer poke several dozen holes through top of cake. Remove from pan when cooled. Glaze.

Glaze:
¼ cup orange juice

¾ cup sugar
½ tsp. vanilla

Mix all ingredients in a small saucepan. Heat until sugar is dissolved and pour over cooled cake.

Tea Cakes

This is a recipe from my grandmother, who made these cookies on a wood stove. The story goes that she put them in a sugar sack and kept them by the back door for my grandfather, whose blacksmith shop was behind the house.

4 cups flour
½ tsp. cream of tartar
2 eggs
1 cup butter, softened
1 cup white sugar
2 tbsp. buttermilk (or sour milk)
1 tsp. baking soda
1 tsp. vanilla
few dashes of mace

Preheat oven to 350°. Dissolve baking soda in buttermilk. Place flour in a large, wide bowl, making a well in the center. Sprinkle cream of tartar over the flour. Put butter and sugar into the dent and work together with a fork, adding eggs, milk mixture, and vanilla. Mix until well blended. Gradually work in the flour using hands (important). Dough will be stiff. Roll out on floured surface and cut with cookie cutter. Bake until edges of cookies begin to brown, about 15 minutes.

German Spice Cake

This is my husband's favorite cake. The recipe was from his mother.

1 cup sugar
½ cup shortening
1 egg
2 cups flour
2 tsp. baking powder
1 tbsp. cocoa
1 tsp. cinnamon
1 tsp. nutmeg
1 tsp. cloves
¼ tsp. salt
1 cup milk

Preheat oven to 350°. Grease and flour loaf pan. Cream sugar and shortening. Add egg and mix well. Combine dry ingredients and add alternately with milk to the creamed mixture. Pour into pan. Bake for 45 minutes. Cool for 5 minutes and remove from pan and frost with Chocolate Mocha Icing.

Chocolate Mocha Icing:
3 tbsp. coffee
1 tbsp. cocoa
½ tsp. vanilla
1 tbsp. butter

Mix together and add enough powdered sugar to thicken and make a spreading consistency.

Velvet Cookies

A favorite at the Golden Visitors Center. Made by our cookie lady.

1 cup shortening
4 tbsp. peanut butter
1 cup powdered sugar
1 egg

2 cups flour
1 ½ tsp. vanilla
½ tsp. baking powder
¼ tsp. salt

Preheat oven to 375°. Cream shortening and peanut butter. Add sugar; cream well. Mix in egg and vanilla. Add flour, salt, baking powder. Roll dough into balls. Flatten balls and top with chocolate star or Hershey kiss. Place on ungreased cookie sheet. When fully baked, they will appear as if not yet baked. If you wish them to be more crisp, bake till slightly browned.

Sherry Cake

Hint: It isn't named after someone whose name is Sherry.

1 box yellow cake mix
4 eggs
1 small box instant vanilla pudding

¾ cup vegetable oil
¾ cup sherry
1 generous tsp. nutmeg

Preheat oven to 350°. Combine all ingredients and mix for 5 minutes. Pour into a well-greased bundt pan. Bake for 50 minutes or until knife inserted in center comes out clean.

Be sure the pan is thoroughly greased, or the cake will stick.

Bananas Foster Cheesecake Squares

This wonderful dessert is for all of us who love the flavor of New Orleans style Bananas Foster, but want to serve it to a crowd. No flames with this dessert, just great taste.

Crust:

2 cups vanilla wafer crumbs

½ cup pecans, toasted and chopped

¼ cup (1/2 stick) unsalted butter or margarine, melted

¼ cup brown sugar

Filling:

24 oz. low-fat cream cheese, softened

½ cup brown sugar

2 tsp. dark rum or rum extract

3 eggs

½ cup mashed ripe banana (1 large)

Cheesecake:

Topping:

2 medium bananas, sliced

2 tsp. lemon juice

1/3 squeeze bottle caramel ice cream topping

½ cup pecan halves, toasted

Crust: Mix all ingredients and press into bottom of 13" x 9" baking pan. Set aside.

Filling: In a mixer bowl, beat together cream cheese, sugar, and rum until smooth. Add eggs, mix just until incorporated. Gently stir in mashed banana. Pour over crust. Bake at 350 ° for 30 minutes or until center is set. Remove from oven and cool. Refrigerate 3 hours or overnight.

Topping: Toss bananas with lemon juice. Drain. Arrange banana slices over cheese-cake. Drizzle caramel syrup evenly over top. Sprinkle with pecans. Cut into squares and serve. Serves 24.

Anginette (Grandma's Italian Cookies)

Cookies:
4 eggs
½ cup sugar
¼ cup butter
4 tsp. vanilla
Lemon juice
3 cups flour
4 tsp. baking powder

Icing:
orange flavor or anisette liquor
powdered sugar
water

Preheat over to 375°. Blend ingredients for cookies together. Roll it into a loaf. Cut into butter-pat size pieces of dough. Bake for 15 minutes.

Make icing using only enough water to form a pourable paste. Ice cookies when they come out of the oven. Cool.

Carrot Cookies

2 cups flour
¾ cup sugar
¾ cup margarine or butter
1 egg

1 cup mashed cooked carrots
1 tsp. baking powder
1 tsp. vanilla
½ cup chopped nuts

Preheat oven to 375°. Mix all ingredients well. Drop by teaspoonful onto a greased cookie sheet. Bake for 15 minutes. Ice while warm.

Icing:
Powdered sugar
Rind of 1 orange
Juice of ½ orange

Mix well - just dip to frost cookie.

Chocolate Chip Shortbread

1 cup butter, softened
1/3 cup sugar
1¾ cups all-purpose flour
¼ cup cornstarch
1 cup mini semi-sweet real chocolate chips

Heat oven to 350°. Combine butter and sugar in large mixer bowl. Beat at medium speed, scraping bowl often, until creamy (1 - 2 minutes.) Reduce speed to low. Add flour and cornstarch; beat, scraping bowl often, until well mixed (1 - 2 minutes.) Stir in chocolate chips by hand. Press into ungreased 13" x 9" baking pan. Prick all over with fork. Bake for 35 - 45 minutes or until edges just begin to brown. (If browning too quickly, cover with aluminum foil.) Cool in pan 15 minutes. Cut into bars while still warm. Makes 36 bars.

Pumpkin Cookies

½ cup butter or margarine
1 ½ cups sugar
1 egg
1 cup cooked or canned pumpkin
1 tsp. vanilla
2 ½ cups all-purpose flour

1 tsp. baking powder
1 tsp. baking soda
½ tsp. salt
1 tsp. nutmeg
1 tsp. cinnamon

Preheat oven to 350°. Cream together butter and sugar. Beat in egg, pumpkin and vanilla. Add flour, baking powder, baking soda, salt, nutmeg and cinnamon. Mix thoroughly. Drop by teaspoonfuls onto well-greased cookie sheets. Bake for 15 minutes or until lightly browned. Makes six dozen cookies.

German Butter Cookies (Buttergeback)

My mother moved to the United States from Germany when she was 27 years old, and brought many of her favorite cookie recipes with her. They have always played an important part in our holiday traditions. I have many fond memories of helping my mother in the kitchen before Christmas time.

3½ cups flour
1¾ cups sugar
1 cup butter
4 egg yolks
grated lemon peel
1 egg yolk and a little milk to make the glaze

Preheat oven to 350°. Mix the ingredients well on a cutting board. Chill in the refrigerator for 1 hour. Roll out the dough on a floured board to 1/8" - ¼" thick. Using cookie cutters, put into various shapes. Arrange on cookie sheets. Brush each cookie lightly with a mixture of egg yolk and a little milk. Decorate with sprinkles for the holidays. Bake until light golden in color.

Spitzbuben (German Linzer Tortes)

This is a very popular traditional German recipe for Christmas cookies. They are time-consuming to bake, but festive and beautiful to look at. If desired, raspberry preserves may be substituted for the red currant jelly.

1¾ cups flour
7/8 cup sugar
1 cup + 1 tbsp. butter
2 eggs
pinch salt
3½ oz. ground hazelnuts or almonds
red currant jelly
powdered sugar

Mix the first 6 ingredients to make the "short crust" dough. Refrigerate for 30 minutes. When chilled, roll out the dough on a floured surface to 1/8" thick. Cut into circles with a round cookie cutter. Using a thimble, cut a small circle from the center of half of the cookies. Chill the cookies for one hour. Bake on a cookie sheet at 325° until golden. Remove from oven.

Spread currant jelly onto the smooth side of the intact cookies, and set the remaining cookies (with the holes) on top, so that the jelly glues the cookies together. Dot a little extra jelly into the hole in the center of each cookie. Dip both sides of the completed sandwich cookies in powdered sugar.

Cowboy Cookies

This moist chocolate chip cookie is named for its large size.

2 extra large eggs
1 cup granulated sugar
1 cup lightly packed brown sugar
1 cup canola oil
1 tsp. vanilla
1 tsp. soda

½ tsp. salt
½ tsp. baking powder
2 cups unsifted flour
2 cups oats
12 oz. chocolate chips
1 cup shredded coconut

Preheat oven to 350°. Beat the first four ingredients on medium speed of mixer until fluffy. Add the vanilla. In another bowl, combine the dry ingredients. Add dry ingredients to the creamed mixture. Drop by ¼ cupfuls onto greased baking sheet. Put 8 mounds of dough to a pan as these cookies will spread. Bake for 10 - 15 minutes. Makes about 20 giant cookies.

Raspberry Strips

1 cup butter
½ cup sugar
2¼ cups flour
seedless raspberry jam

Frosting:
1 cup powdered sugar
2 tsp. almond extract
water enough to thin

Preheat oven to 350°. Cream butter and sugar together. Add flour. Mix together until dough holds together. Divide dough into 8 equal parts. Shape each part into a strip 8 x 2 x ½" thick. Place strips on cookie sheets, 4 to a sheet. Make a shallow indentation down the middle of each strip and fill with raspberry jam. Bake for 18 - 20 minutes. Remove from oven and drizzle with frosting. While warm, cut diagonally into 1" strips. Makes 5 dozen strips.

Almond Meringues

These are fabulous crowd-pleasers. The butter cookie base adds a rich texture to the melt-in-your-mouth meringue.

½ cup butter
3 tbsp. sugar
3 eggs, separated
¾ cup flour
1/8 tsp. salt
¾ cup sugar
1 tsp. vanilla
1 tsp. cinnamon
½ cup shredded almonds

Preheat oven to 325°. Grease cookie sheets.

Cookie base: Beat butter until soft. Cream in 3 tablespoons sugar. Beat in egg yolks. Blend in flour until consistency is even and dough is workable. Roll to ¼" thickness and cut into 1½" circles. Place on cookie sheet about 1½" apart.

Meringue: Whip egg whites until stiff. Add sugar and salt. Fold in vanilla, cinnamon, and almonds. Place a heaping teaspoon of the meringue on each cookie base. Bake for 12 minutes or until meringue develops a light crust. Makes about 3 dozen.

If you are baking multiple batches, prepare the trays one at a time, keeping meringue refrigerated until needed. It will lose its peak if it gets too warm.

Chocolate Zucchini Cake

1 cup brown sugar
½ cup sugar
½ cup margarine
½ cup oil
3 eggs
1 tsp. vanilla
½ cup buttermilk
2 ½ cups flour

½ tsp. allspice
½ tsp. cinnamon
½ tsp. salt
2 tsp. soda
4 tbsp. cocoa
3 zucchini, grated (at least 6" long)
1 cup chocolate chips

Preheat oven to 325°. Grease and flour a 9" x 13" pan. Cream together in a large bowl the brown sugar, sugar, margarine, and oil. Add eggs, vanilla, and buttermilk and mix well. Sift together in a large bowl the flour, allspice, cinnamon, salt, soda, cocoa. Add grated zucchini to the creamed mixture. Next add dry ingredients and mix. Pour into pan. Sprinkle chocolate chips on top. Bake for 45 to 55 minutes or until toothpick inserted in center comes out clean.

Grandma's Cheesecake

16 oz. cottage cheese
16 oz. cream cheese
6 tbsp. flour
1½ cups sugar

4 large eggs
1 tbsp. vanilla
1 stick of butter, melted
16 oz. sour cream

Preheat oven to 325°. Prepare a 9-inch springform pan by lining the bottom with a 9" circle of waxed or parchment paper and running a rectangular strip of paper up the side. In a food processor cream cottage cheese and cream cheese. Add flour, then sugar. Beat in eggs, vanilla and melted butter. Mix well. Add sour cream. Pour into pan. Bake for 1 hour. Turn off oven and do not open door. Let the cheesecake stand in the oven for 1 more hour.

Variations: If you desire a crust, combine crushed graham crackers or chocolate cookie crumbs and enough butter to make a crust paste and press into pan. For a lower-cholesterol version, use 2 egg whites but no yolks, for each egg.

Southwest Cheesecake

Mesquite meal, prickly pear nectar, and mesquite honey are all available from Native Seed/Search at www.nativeseeds.org. If you don't care for the mesquite meal, increase graham cracker crumbs to 1 ½ cups.

1 cup graham cracker crumbs	3 large eggs
½ cup mesquite meal	2 peaches, ripe
2/3 cup mesquite honey, divided	
6 tbsp. butter, melted	**Prickly Pear Glaze:**
½ tsp. cinnamon	¾ cup apple juice
2 tsp. vanilla	2 tbsp. cornstarch
1 cup sour cream	2/3 cup prickly pear nectar
24 ounces cream cheese, softened	1/3 cup mesquite honey

Preheat oven to 350°. In a medium bowl combine graham cracker crumbs, mesquite meal, 1 tbsp honey, and cinnamon. Using fingers, press into bottom and sides of a 9-inch spring form pan. Set aside. In a large bowl, beat together cream cheese, honey, and vanilla until creamy. Beat in eggs one at a time just until combined. Do not over beat or cheese-cake will crack. Stir in sour cream. Pour batter over crust. Bake 50 to 60 minutes or until center is just set. Turn oven off, leaving door slightly ajar. Leave cake in the oven for 1 hour, then remove and cool. Chill at least 2 hours, then prepare topping. Peel and slice peaches, arrange on top of cake. Pour glaze over peaches and allow to drip down sides of cake. Chill until serving time.

Glaze:

Combine ¼ cup apple juice and cornstarch, set aside. In a saucepan combine remaining juice, nectar and honey. Stir over medium heat until honey melts. Add cornstarch mixture and stir until mixture boils and thickens. Cook one minute more then set aside and cool.

Pumpkin Cheesecake Bars

These rich and creamy bars are a big hit at our annual cemetery tours!

1 16 oz. pkg. pound cake mix
3 eggs
8 oz. cream cheese, softened
16 oz. pumpkin pureé
1 cup chopped nuts
2 tbsp. butter, softened
4 tsp. pumpkin pie spice
1 14 oz. can sweetened condensed milk
½ tsp. salt

Preheat oven to 350°. In a large bowl mix (on low) cake mix, 1 egg, butter, and 2 teaspoons pumpkin pie spice until crumbly. Press onto the bottom of a 13" x 9" x 2" pan. In a large bowl beat cream cheese until fluffy. Gradually add the can of sweetened condensed milk, then remaining 2 eggs, pumpkin pureé, pumpkin spice and salt. Mix well. Pour over crust; sprinkle with nuts, and bake 25 - 30 minutes or until firm. Cool and chill. Cut into squares. Store in refrigerator.

Golden Specialties

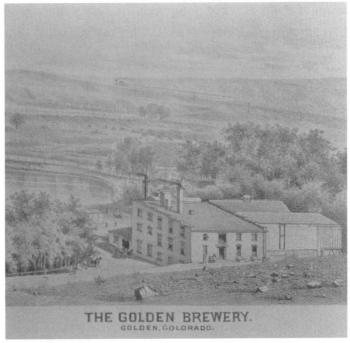

THE GOLDEN BREWERY.
GOLDEN, COLORADO.

Co-founded by Adolph Coors and Jacob Schueler in 1873, Coors Brewing Company is the very essence of the American dream. The November 12, 1873, edition of the *Colorado Transcript* noted that: *Another new and extensive manufacturey is about to be added to the number already in Golden. Messers J. Scheuler (sic) and Adolph Coors, of Denver, have purchased the old tannery property of C.C. Welch and John Pipe, and will convert it into a brewery. They propose making large additions to the building, making it into one of the most extensive works of its kind in the territory...."* Golden's historic brewery, the largest single-site operation in the world, offers tours 6 days a week, and a tasting room.

(Photo: Coors Brewing Company engraving; courtesy of the Golden Pioneer Museum)

Cherry Bounce

George West, a Union Army Captain and one of Golden's founders, settled a disagreement with a Confederate sympathizer over glasses of this concoction. Make at Your Own Risk!

Take ½ gallon wild (or tame) cherries, and put in a 5 gallon crock. Add the same amount of water and one pound of sugar. Mash well. Add 1 qt. brandy and let it set for about 4 months, mashing and stirring with a wooden spoon from time to time. Strain seeds and pulp, and pour liquid into jars, seal, and let rest for another month, then sip slowly!

Ginger Beer (Non-Alcoholic)

Fresh ginger root, about 2.5 inches long
Juice of 1 lemon
1 cup sugar
1 tsp. dry yeast
1 tsp. cream of tartar

Smash the ginger root (one good whack with a rolling pin) and add it to 2 quarts boiling water along with the lemon juice and the sugar. When mixture cools to lukewarm, add yeast and cream of tartar. Stir until yeast dissolves. Cover and let stand overnight. In the morning, pour liquid into clean bottles and cork for old-timey effect. Leave sediment in pan. Let bottles stand at room temperature for 3 – 4 days until fermented. Chill, then enjoy.

Warning: If left to ferment too long, beverage will blow cork out. Check after 2 days to see if it's bubbly, chill as soon as it reaches this stage.

Dill Pickles

Brine:
13 cups water
1 quart cider vinegar (5% acidity)
1 cup pickling salt

1 bushel mixed run pickling cucumbers
fresh dill
garlic cloves, peeled
Oriental peppers

You must use pickling cucumbers. Do not use burpless, seedless, or other type of cucumber. One bushel of mixed run cucumbers will give you about 36 quarts of pickles. When you get mixed run cucumbers, you can sort them by size and have a variety of pickles: small, whole, sliced, chunk and spears. The fresher the cucumber, the crisper the pickle. Before packing in the cucumbers, place in the bottom of the jar: small, dried, hot, red chili peppers, fresh garlic and sprigs of fresh dill. The peppers are sometimes called Oriental or Japanese peppers. They are an inch to an inch and a half long. You can choose the amount that appeals to your taste. For regular pickles use 1 pepper, 1 sprig of dill and 1 clove of garlic. For extra spicy pickles, triple the amounts of garlic and pepper. You can use cayenne pepper flakes if you can't find the hot peppers – ½ teaspoon equals one pepper. Bring brine ingredients to a boil and pour over hot, sterile, packed jars of cucumbers. Seal with flats and rings and process in a hot water bath appropriate for your altitude. If you are unsure about this process, call the County Extension Office for a pamphlet.

Note: This brine can be used to pickle any vegetable. I have had great success with okra, jalapenos and garlic. You can use the brine alone or in any combination of dill, hot peppers and garlic.

Lookout Mountain Nature Center

910 Colorow Road
Golden, CO 80401
303.526.0323
http://openspace.jeffco.us

Lookout Mountain Nature Center (LMNC) was housed humbly first in a room, then garage, and then servant's house of the Boettcher Mansion. In 1997, a beautiful new visitor/nature center opened its doors. The facility demonstrates sustainable design by using earth-friendly building products including floors from recycled train boxcars, decking of recycled soda bottles and sawdust, floor tiles from recycled windshields, locally quarried rock, native plant landscaping and more!

Quick Dill Pickles

This is a fun recipe that's great for kids to make. We use it in our "Life in the Old West" field school, where kids learn how to make some pioneer treats. The pickles are not suitable for canning, so refrigerate after making.

6 small cucumbers	1 tsp. salt
1 small bunch fresh dill	¼ cup sugar
12 whole black peppercorns	1 garlic clove, thinly sliced
1 cup white wine vinegar	

In a large bowl, mix together all ingredients. Store in refrigerator in covered containers or jars.

Eggless, Milkless, Butterless Cake

This recipe comes from Royal Baking Powder's 1917 book 55 Ways to Save Eggs.

½ cup butter	2 cups flour
1 cup brown sugar	2 tsp. Royal baking powder
2 eggs	1 tsp. nutmeg
1 cup milk	1 tsp. cinnamon
1 cup raisins	½ tsp. salt
2 oz. citron, cut fine	

Preheat oven to 350º. Boil sugar, liquid, fruit, shortening, salt, and spices together in a saucepan for 3 minutes. When cool, add flour and baking powder which have been sifted together. Mix well, bake in a loaf pan for 45 minutes and top with white icing made from confectioner's sugar, butter, vanilla, and milk.

Raisin Cake

2 cups raisins
2 cups water
1 cup sugar
½ cup shortening
1 or 2 eggs
1 tsp. cinnamon

½ tsp. allspice
pinch of cloves
pinch of salt
2 cups flour
1 tsp. baking soda

Boil water and raisins until one cup liquid remains. Cream sugar and shortening and add eggs. Add sifted dry ingredients alternately with raisin liquid. Add raisins and bake 45 minutes at 350º. Instructions with this recipe were as follows: If you do not have ground spices, boil whole spices in a bag with the raisins. Save all dabs of fruit such as apple, pickled peach juice, or others and add. This cake keeps well if you hide it.

Molasses Drop Cakes

This wood stove recipe was adapted from The 1896 Boston Cooking School Cook Book by Fannie Merritt Farmer.

1 cup molasses
½ cup melted butter
1 cup sugar
2 tsp. soda
1 cup hot water

1 egg
2 tsp. ginger
½ tsp. salt
4 cups flour

Preheat oven to 350°. Mix molasses, butter, and sugar. Add soda and beat thoroughly; then add water, egg well beaten, and flour mixed and sifted with ginger and salt. Drop by spoonfuls on a buttered sheet. Bake twelve to fifteen minutes.

Lookout Mountain Nature Center

Continued

LMNC is part of the Jefferson County Open Space program and offers something for everyone. Connect with nature on the 110-acre preserve by strolling trails winding through forest and meadow or picnic beneath towering pine trees. Join a naturalist to discover natural treasures at LMNC on guided programs. Inside the visitor/nature center, explore interactive exhibits that reveal some of nature's secrets. Visit the Discovery Corner and Observation Room.

The Nature Center hours are Tuesday through Sunday 10:00 a.m. to 4:00 p.m. and from Memorial Day to Labor Day the center is open 9:00 a.m. to 5:00 p.m. on weekends. The Preserve is open from 8:00 a.m. to dusk daily.

Sourdough Starter

What Western cookbook would be complete without a sourdough recipe? Prior to the advent of the Union-Pacific Transcontinental Railroad, settlers came west in small groups or in large wagon trains. Six weeks was the average travel time from "jumping off" points such as St. Joseph's, Missouri, to points west like Denver or Salt Lake City. Fresh food was in short supply by the time Week 3 rolled around. Sourdough became an indispensable part of any journey. Neither milk nor eggs are required, both items very expensive and in extremely short supply.

In a large saucepan, boil 2 unpeeled potatoes until they begin to fall apart in the saucepan. Skim out skins. Do not drain. Mash potatoes thoroughly. Cool. Add water to make 2 cups, if necessary. Add 2 tbsp. sugar and 2 cups flour. If desired, add ½ tsp. yeast to speed fermentation. Beat all ingredients until smooth. Put into sourdough pot, or large ceramic crock, with room for the sponge to expand. Cover loosely with cheesecloth or foil. Set aside in a warm place to ferment – maintain a constant temperature.

Your sourdough will be ready to use anywhere from 10 hours to 1 month (or 1 year) later. When you use it depends on your personal tastes; the longer it ferments, the more mellow the flavor. To speed along the process, add 1 tsp. sugar and 1 tbsp. flour. Make certain there is enough water to keep it from becoming too thick. This will become the starter for all future batches of sourdough. When ready to use it, stir through it with a wooden spoon. Stir out all lumps. If it is stiff and heavy, add water to make it a thick, creamy sponge. When feeding your starter (adding flour and sugar) feed it at least 10 hours before you plan to use it.

When you use the starter, be certain to replenish it with additional sugar and flour. Always reserve 1 cup of sponge to provide the starter for the next batch. A starter can be made to go dormant by storing in the refrigerator; just pull it out and let it warm up for 10 – 12 hours before using.

Sourdough Bread

2 cups sourdough starter
2 tbsp. dry yeast
4 cups lukewarm water
1 tbsp. salt
3 eggs
¼ cup melted shortening
¼ cup sugar
12 cups white flour
1 tsp. soda

Dissolve yeast in water with part of sugar added. Let set ½ hour or so. Add starter and mix well. Add eggs, salt, remaining sugar and shortening and some flour. Beat well to thoroughly mix and develop gluten. Add more of the flour with soda and beat well. Add enough flour to make dough workable; knead until smooth. Let rise until double. Punch down and let rise again. Shape into loaves (6 – 7 loaves). Let rise to above top of pan. Bake at 350° about 40 minutes or until well done.

Sourdough Waffles

2 cups sourdough starter
2 tbsp. sugar
4 tbsp. oil
1 egg
½ tsp. salt
1 tsp. baking soda

Heat waffle iron. In a large bowl, fold together starter, sugar, egg, oil and salt. Dilute baking soda in 1 tsp. water. Stir well. Fold soda water into batter. The batter will begin to thicken and double in volume as you stir. Begin pouring waffles immediately Cook until desired degree of doneness is reached.

Sourdough Blueberry Muffins

1 cup sourdough starter	½ tsp. soda
½ cup sugar	1 tsp. baking powder
4 tbsp. oil	1 tsp. grated lemon rind
1 egg	1 cup blueberries
2 cups flour	

In a large bowl, blend sourdough, egg, and oil. Sift in dry ingredients; fold together gently. Dust blueberries with a little bit of flour. This will keep them from sinking to the bottom of the muffin. Fold into batter. Fill muffin cups or well-greased muffin tins half-full. Bake at 400° for 25 minutes or until golden brown.

Quaker Muffins

This recipe is adapted from The 1896 Boston Cooking-School Cook Book, written for wood stove cooking. We have updated it for the modern oven.

2/3 cup rolled oats	½ tsp. salt
1½ cups flour	1 cup scalded milk
3 tbsp. sugar	1 egg
3 tbsp. baking powder	1 tbsp. melted butter

Preheat oven to 400°. Prepare muffin pan with liners or grease with shortening. Turn scalded milk on rolled oats, let stand five minutes; add sugar, salt, and melted butter; sift in flour and baking powder, mix thoroughly and add egg well beaten. Bake for 15-20 minutes or until a tester comes out clean.

Eugenia Mitchell's Sheepherders Bread

Eugenia Mitchell, founder of the Rocky Mountain Quilt Museum, was born in Brazil in 1903 where her parents, John and Theodora Mueller Hartmeister, were missionaries of the Lutheran Church. Upon their return to the States, Eugenia grew up as a "tomboy" in Storm Lake, Iowa. She would rather climb trees than quilt, but her mother quilted, and Eugenia's interest grew as she made quilts for the family.

3 cups very hot water
½ cup butter or shortening
½ cup sugar
2½ tsp. salt

2 packages yeast
9 cups flour, wheat or white
salad oil

Combine water, sugar and salt, add butter and let melt. Cool to 115° then stir in yeast and let set in warm place 15 minutes. Add 5 cups flour; beat until smooth. Batter may be divided into two bowls. Add 2½ cups whole wheat flour to one bowl, and 2½ cups white flour to the other. Knead on breadboard until smooth, about 10 minutes. Return dough to bowls and let rise 1½ hours. Punch down on floured board and form a smooth ball. Place in a greased Dutch oven with greased lid. Let rise in warm place about 30 minutes. Raise lid. Preheat oven to 375°. Bake covered with lid for 12 minutes. Remove lid and continue baking for 30 – 35 minutes, or until it sounds hollow and is a golden brown. Makes 1 very large single loaf, or 2 loaves if 1 is white and 1 is whole wheat.

Friends of Dinosaur Ridge

Continued

Today, the Friends consist of nearly 400 members and approximately 100 volunteers. Every year, the Friends give guided programs to over 11,000 people and another 33,000 people visit the Visitor's Center located off Alameda Parkway near Red Rocks Park.

Admission to Dinosaur Ridge and the Visitor's Center is free and donations are gratefully accepted. Hours of operation are Monday through Saturday from 9:00am to 4:00pm, and Sundays from noon to 4:00pm.

Rice Muffins

This recipe is adapted from The 1896 Boston Cooking-School Cook Book, written for wood stove cooking. We have updated it for the modern oven.

2½ cups butter
1 cup cooked rice
4 tsp. baking powder
½ tsp. salt
1 cup milk
1 egg
¼ cup melted butter

Preheat oven to 400°. Mix and sift flour, salt, and baking powder, work in rice with tips of fingers; and gradually add milk, egg well beaten, and butter. Bake in buttered muffin rings placed in buttered pan or buttered gem pans for 15-20 minutes or until a tester comes out clean. .

Hardtack

In honor of our Civil War re-enactors.

5 cups flour
1½ cups water
1 tsp. salt

Mix ingredients in a big blob. Sprinkle with flour so that it doesn't stick too badly. Knead well and roll ¼" thick. Cut into 3½" squares. Pierce each square with 16 evenly spaced holes. Bake at 350° for one or more hours until it repels musket balls.

Warning: dunk in black coffee to reduce the trauma to your teeth; it will also drive any weevils to the top of the cup (this helps to count calories, as weevils are "protein" and not "starch").

Black Bean Soup

This is adapted from The 1896 Boston Cooking-School Cook Book.

1 pint black beans
2 quarts cold water
2 stalks celery or ¼ tsp. celery salt
½ tbsp. salt
1/8 tsp. pepper
¼ tsp. mustard

few grains cayenne pepper
3 tbsp. butter
1 ½ tbsp. flour
2 hard boiled eggs
1 lemon

Soak beans overnight; in the morning drain and add cold water. Slice onion and cook five minutes with half the butter, adding to beans, with celery stalks broken in pieces. Simmer three or four hours, or until beans are soft; add more water as water boils away. Rub through a sieve, reheat to the boiling point, and add salt, pepper, mustard, and cayenne well mixed. Bind with remaining butter and flour cooked together. Cut eggs in thin slices, and lemon in thin slices, removing seeds. Put in tureen, and strain the soup over them.

Apple Tapioca Pudding

This recipe is adapted from The Boston Cooking School Cook Book by Mrs. D. A. Lincoln, 1884. It was created for a wood stove; we have adapted it slightly for modern ovens.

¾ cup pearl tapioca
1 quart boiling water
½ tsp. salt

7 apples, cored and pared
lemon juice
sugar

Pick over and wash pearl tapioca. Pour the boiling water over it and cook in the double boiler till transparent; stir often, and add salt. Preheat oven to 350º. Put the cored apples in a round baking dish, and fill the cores with sugar and lemon juice. Pour the tapioca over them and bake till the apples are very soft. Serve hot or cold, with sugar and cream.

A delicious variation may be made by using half pears, or canned quinces, and half apples.

C. V. Wood's World Championship Chili

C.V. Wood Jr. was one of the world's foremost theme park creators, his work was instrumental in creating and perpetuating the early history of this industry. This is his 1969 award-winning recipe.

1 3-pound stewing chicken, cut into pieces
1 quart water or 2 10-ounce cans chicken broth
1/4 cup Wesson oil
4 lbs. flank steak
5 lbs. thin, center-cut pork shops
6 long green chilies, peeled
2 tsp. sugar
3 tsp. ground oregano
3 tsp. ground cumin
1 tsp. MSG (optional)
3 tsp. pepper
4 tsp. salt

5 tbsp. Gebbhardt chili powder
1 tsp. cilantro, also known as Chinese parsley
1 tsp. thyme
8 ounces Budweiser beer
4 15-ounce cans Hunts Tomatoes
1/2 cup celery, finely chopped
2 cloves garlic, finely chopped
3 medium onions, cut into * inch pieces
2 green peppers, cut into 3/8 inch pieces
1 pound Jack cheese, grated
1 lime
dash of Tabasco sauce

Combine chicken with water in a large pot and simmer 2 hours. Strain off broth and reserve chicken for other use, or use canned chicken broth. Trim all fat and bones from pork and cut it into 1 inch cubes. Trim all fat from flank steak and cut it into 3/8 inch cubes. Boil chilies 15 minutes or until tender. Remove seeds and cut the chilies into 1/2 inch squares. Mix sugar, oregano, cumin, MSG, pepper, salt, chili powder, cilantro and thyme with beer until all lumps are dissolved. Add the tomatoes, celery, chilies, beer mixture and garlic to the chicken broth.

Pour about a third of the oil into a skillet, add pork and brown. Cook only half total amount at a time. Add the pork to the broth mixture, cook slowly 30 minutes. Brown beef in the remaining oil, about one third of the total amount at a time. Add the beef to the pork mixture and cook slowly about 1 hour. Add onions and peppers. Simmer 2 – 3 hours until meat is broken down, stirring with a wooden spoon every 15 – 20 minutes. Cool 1 hour and refrigerate 24 hours. Reheat chili before serving it. About 5 minutes before serving time, add grated cheese. Just before serving, add the juice of the lime and stir the mixture with a wooden spoon. Makes 6 quarts.

Cream Slaw

This recipe comes from one of Golden's pioneer families.

1 gallon cabbage, cut fine
1 pint sour cream
1 tsp. flour
2 eggs
1 tbsp. black pepper
1 piece butter, size walnut
1 pint vinegar
½ cup sugar
1 tbsp. salt
1 tbsp. mustard

Put vinegar, sugar and butter in a saucepan and let boil; stir eggs, cream and flour, previously well mixed, into the vinegar and coil thoroughly; throw over the cabbage previously sprinkled with salt, pepper and mustard. Mix.

Try diluting vinegar with one fourth water, cut down on pepper, partially cool dressing before adding to cabbage.

Cocoanut Custard

This recipe appeared in the June 6, 1907 edition of the Colorado Transcript.

Bring 1 quart of milk to scald. Remove from heat and add 3 egg yolks, and 3 tbsp. sugar. Stir well. Return to heat and thicken with 1 tbsp. cornstarch and 1 cup shredded cocoanut. When thick, pour into dishes. Whip 3 egg whites to stiff froth and spread over top of dishes. Bake in hot oven until brown.

In the Time Before

Long before fur trappers, gold seekers, and settlers ever ventured out onto the Plains, the area in and around Golden was home to the First People of the Americas. For over 12,000 years people from many Native American groups hunted and camped in the valley. They hunted mammoth, buffalo, and pronghorn; they collected chokecherry, yucca, and wild onions; and they left behind their tools, pottery, jewelry, and sometimes their homes.

Cornish Pasty

Many of Colorado's gold and coal miners came from Cornwall, England. They brought this wonderful dish with them.

Crust:
6 cups sifted flour
1 tbsp. salt
1 1/3 cups shortening
2/3 to ¾ cup water

Cornish Pasty Filling:
2½ pounds boneless shoulder steak
¼ pound lean pork
1½ cups coarsely chopped onion
6 cups thinly sliced raw potatoes
2 tbsp. salt
1 tsp. pepper

Preheat oven to 425°. Sift flour and salt together. Cut in shortening until particles are size of peas. Add enough water to hold dough together when lightly pressed. Roll dough on lightly floured surface to a circle 18 inches in diameter. Carefully slip onto greased baking sheet. Remove tendons and membrane from steak. Trim off excess fat, but not all. Cut meat in bite-size pieces. Combine with remaining ingredients. Place Cornish Pasty filling onto half of the circle. Moisten edges with water; fold over to form a semi-circle. Seal edges. Cut eight steam vents. Bake for one hour and fifteen minutes. Yield: 8 – 10 portions.

Silverheels' Sizzling Crab Empanadas

From 1992 to the late 1990's the Silverheels restaurant occupied the Loveland Block at 1122 Washington Avenue. It was the second Silverheels, run by proprietor Bob Starekow. The original restaurant still operates in Frisco today.

6 oz. cream cheese
6 oz. pepper jack cheese
½ lb. crab meat
½ tsp. cumin
1 tsp. coriander
2 tbsp. onion, chopped
1 tbsp. minced garlic
1 egg, beaten
1 tbsp. bread crumbs
72 wonton wrappers
water for spray bottles
frying oil, as needed

Soften and whip cream cheese until soft and fluffy. Grate jack cheese and mix with cream cheese. Add crab, spices, minced onion, garlic, and beaten egg. Add bread crumbs to tighten. Mix well and set aside. Lay 36 wonton skins on the counter side by side. Drop one teaspoon full of the crab mixture in the center of each skin. Spray water over all sides to moisten. Top each with a second wonton skin and press down around the filling of each empanada to seal. Spray water over all once again to moisten. Finish empanada by bringing four corners together at the top and pinching together with your fingertips to seal. Heat oil to 375° and fry empanadas six at a time until golden brown. Serve with a prepared Chinese duck sauce and a Mexican salsa. Serves 6.

In the Time Before

Continued

The Golden area has many wonderful archaeological sites that have been excavated and recorded over the years. Among these are Magic Mountain, dating back about 8000 years, and Hall-Woodland Cave, about 1500 years old. We don't know for certain who these people were, but presume they were the ancestors of today's Ute, Comanche, and Apache tribes. Many of the items recovered from the excavations can be viewed at the Golden Pioneer Museum and other museums in eastern Colorado.

Scalloped Eggs

This was adapted from The 1896 Cooking School Cook Book by Fannie Merritt Farmer, designed for wood fire cooking.

6 hard boiled eggs
1 pint White Sauce
¾ cup chopped cold meat
¾ cup buttered cracker crumbs

White Sauce:
2 tbsp. butter
2 tbsp. flour
1 cup milk
¼ tsp. salt
Few grains of pepper

Chop eggs finely. Sprinkle bottom of a buttered baking dish with crumbs, cover with one half the eggs, eggs with sauce, and sauce with meat; repeat. Cover with remaining crumbs. Place in oven on center grate, and bake until crumbs are brown. Ham is the best meat to use for this dish. Chicken, veal, or fish may be used.

Sauce: Put butter in sauce pan, stir until melted and bubbling; add flour mixed with seasonings, and stir until thoroughly blended. Pour on gradually the milk, adding about one-third at a time, stirring until well mixed, then beating until smooth and glossy. If a wire whisk is used, all the milk may be added at once; and although more quickly made if milk is scalded, it is not necessary.

Squash Pie

Please note that these recipes are written for a wood burning stove. They include no indications for baking temperatures and sometimes no indication of baking time. This is adapted from The 1896 Boston Cooking School Cook Book.

1¼ cups steamed and strained squash	½ tsp. salt
¼ cup sugar	1 egg
¼ tsp. cinnamon, ginger or nutmeg	7/8 cup milk
or ½ tsp. lemon extract	

Mix sugar, salt, and spice or extract. Add squash, egg slightly beaten and milk gradually. Bake in one crust, following directions for Custard Pie (below). If richer pie is desired, use one cup squash, one-half cup each of milk and cream, and an additional egg yolk.

Instructions for Custard Pie: Line plate with paste, and build up a fluted rim. Strain in the mixture and sprinkle with a few gratings nutmeg. Bake in quick oven at first to set rim, decrease the heat afterwards, as egg and milk in combination need to be cooked at low temperature.

Apple Crisp

This recipe is best prepared over a campfire or on a wood stove.

Best made in an iron Dutch oven. I prefer a #10 or #12.

Grease the inside bottom and sides of Dutch oven with butter. Start with 5 – 10 lbs. of apples peeled, washed and cut into medium size chunks. Fill the Dutch oven, leaving about 2 inches on top. Pre-soften 2 sticks of butter. Mix ½ cup butter (about 2 sticks), 2 cups of sugar, ¾ cup of flour and a teaspoon of cinnamon until the dry goods are all mixed into the softened butter. Spread the mixture over the top of the apples and cover.

Place on a fire that has burned down to coals. Be careful not to use too hot a fire. Place some coals on top of the Dutch oven. Cook for 35 – 45 minutes or until applies are soft. Let cool and serve with heavy cream poured on top. Enjoy!

Eugenia Mitchell's Fruit & Zucchini Bars

¾ cup butter or oleo
½ cup brown sugar
½ cup white sugar
2 eggs
1 tsp. vanilla
1 cup whole wheat flour
¾ cup white flour
1 ½ tsp. baking powder
½ tsp. salt
¾ cup shredded coconut
¾ cup snipped dates
¾ cup raisins
2 cups zucchini peeled and grated (2 7" zucchini)

Preheat oven at 350°. Grease a 10" x 15" jellyroll pan. Beat together the butter and sugar until creamy. Add eggs and vanilla and beat until well blended. Add flour, baking powder and salt and mix well. Stir in the coconut, dates, raisins and zucchini. Spread mixture in the greased pan and bake for 35 – 40 minutes. Cool slightly on a rack.

Frosting:

1 tbsp. melted butter
1 tsp. vanilla
1 cup powdered sugar
2 tsp. milk
½ tsp. cinnamon
¼ tsp. nutmeg
1 cup nuts, chopped

Beat together until smooth then spread on warm bars. Sprinkle with nuts.

George West's Lemon Custard

This recipe appeared in the Colorado Transcript, June 14, 1876. It comes from one of Golden's founders, George West. It has not been tested by our committee.

Juice and rind of 1 lemon
1 cup of sugar
2 egg yolks
3 tbsp. flour
½ pint milk

Line the plates with paste and pour in this custard. While baking, beat two egg whites very stiff; add 2 tablespoons powdered sugar, and spread over the pie when done and brown slightly in the oven.

Original recipe text

"In our bachelor days in Colorado, and occasionally upon the 'tented field' our heart would involuntarily go out to our old landlady of the long ago, as we thought longingly of the delicious lemon custards with which it was her joy to tickle our palate. This was her recipe, which we modestly recommend to housekeepers hereaway: The juice and rind of one lemon, one cup of sugar, the yolk of two eggs, three tablespoonfuls of flour, one-half pint of milk; line the plates with paste and pour in this custard; while baking, beat the whites of two eggs very stiff, add two tablespoonfuls of powdered sugar, and spread over the pie when done and brown slightly in the oven."

Dolly Varden Cake

The following recipe takes its name from Dolly Varden, the delightful character in Dickens' Barnaby Rudge. Dolly's popularity encouraged fashions as well as food. In the 1870's the "Dolly Varden" dress and hat emerged, as well as this delicious cake.

2 cups sugar
1 cup milk
4 eggs, separated
¼ tsp. salt
1 cup butter or margarine
3 ½ cups flour, sifted
3 tsp. baking powder
1 tsp. vanilla

Cream the butter and sugar. Beat in egg yolks, one at a time. Sift flour with baking powder and salt, and add to creamed mixture alternately with milk, beginning and ending with the flour mixture. Add vanilla and fold in stiffly beaten egg whites. Divide batter into three equal parts and to one add:

½ tsp. ground cloves
1 tsp. cinnamon
¼ tsp. nutmeg
½ cup raisins or currants
¼ cup candied citron, if desired

Pour into 3 greased and floured layer pans. Bake at 350° for 20 minutes or until cakes test done. Remove from pans and cool. Put layers together with your favorite seedless jelly, such as raspberry; spice layer in the middle. Frost with a butter cream frosting.

Colorado Wild

Dinosaur Tracks On W. Alameda Ave. Near Mt. Morrison, Colo. Over Sixty Million Years Old

Nearly 100 million years ago, dinosaurs such as the plant-eating Iguanadon and meat-eating Ornithomimus walked the shores of an ancient seaway that covered much of Colorado. Their footprints, left in the moist sands along the shoreline, were miraculously preserved and are now an attraction for dinosaur fanatics both young and old. However, Dinosaur Ridge is more than just dinosaur tracks. During your visit look for impressions of ripple marks, branch impressions from mangrove trees, and burrows left by shore-dwelling animals. On the West side of the Ridge see and touch dinosaur bones left by Colorado's state fossil, the Stegosaurus, almost 150 million years ago.

(Photo: Dinosaur Ridge tracks; courtesy of the Golden Pioneer Museum)

Antelope Onion Stew & Coming to Iron

This recipe came from the Colorado Transcript, March 2, 1892 as related by Edward L. Berthoud. It was created by Bill Campbell in February 1861. The text of the original article is included. We don't recommend trying this at home!

20 lbs. potatoes and Mexican onions
Antelope
Dried apples

Stew antelope meat with onions over open fire. Bake potatoes as side. Stew apples over open fire in a gold pan, until well colored black by the iron rust.

Original Recipe Text:

"Well do I remember in February 1861, carrying up in a bag on my shoulders from Golden to Idaho, twenty pounds of potatoes and Mexican onions costing twenty cents a pound. With this welcome addition to our miners' fare, we reveled in Antelope onion stew and baked potatoes, ending in a dessert of dried apples stewed in a gold pan, and well colored black by the iron rust. Bill Campbell, our baching companion used to call this dessert "coming to iron."

Camp Deer and Corn Fritters

When an old time hunting party "dressed" a deer, nothing went to waste. This recipe has been adapted to a more modern audience.

Hanging rib meat of one deer, washed
    (May use any brisket or flank as well)
4 medium potatoes, washed
2 cobs field corn
1 - 16 oz. can of salsa
cooking oil
salt and pepper

Prepare fire, grease a Dutch oven, heat the pan while the fire is still pretty hot. Salt and pepper the meat, then brown on all sides. Move the pan to a cooler portion of the fire, preferably the coals. Add the salsa and potatoes and corn. Cover. Pile coals on top of the Dutch oven if you have the style with the recessed top. Cook for one hour, making sure the coals stay hot (too hot to put your bare hand closer than 4 inches). Reserve 4 tablespoons of cooked corn for fritters. Serves 4 hungry hunters.

Corn Fritters
4 tbsp. corn, removed from cob
1 tsp. melted fat
1 tsp. baking soda
1 egg
½ cup buttermilk
1 cup flour
½ tsp. salt
additional fat for frying

Begin heating fat in skillet. Mix all ingredients to make a lumpy batter. Drop spoonfuls into hot fat from a safe distance. Makes 4 large or 8 small fritters, enough to feed those same 4 hunters.

Foothills Art Center

Golden's First Presbyterian Church was given land to build a structure in 1871 by town father William A. H. Loveland. The modified Gothic style structure was dedicated in 1872. The church has since built a new home, but the original structure and adjoining parsonage were placed on the National Register of Historic Places and are now home to the Foothills Art Center.

Irish Roast Goose with Potato Stuffing

1 wild goose (8 - 10 lbs.)
1 tsp. salt
¼ tsp. pepper

Stuffing:
10 medium sized, boiled potatoes, riced
1 tbsp. butter
1 cup chopped onions
½ cup chopped celery
4 slices bread, crumbled
1/4 pound ground salt pork
2 eggs, beaten
1 tsp. poultry seasoning
1 tsp. salt
¼ tsp. pepper

Clean the goose, wash thoroughly and pat dry. Rub cavity and outside with salt and pepper mixture.

Stuffing: Boil the potatoes, drain and save the potato water for basting the goose. Rice the potatoes.

Melt butter in skillet and partially cook onions and celery, but do not brown. Add to riced potatoes, bread crumbs, salt pork, eggs, poultry seasoning, salt and pepper. Stuff the goose with potato stuffing and close the cavity. Roast in an uncovered roaster in a 325° oven about 4 hours, or until tender, basting from time to time with potato water.

Canada Goose

1 wild goose
¼ cup salad oil
1 tsp. salt
¼ tsp. pepper
4 tbsp. flour
½ tsp. tarragon
¼ tsp. thyme

¼ lb. salt pork or 6 strips
   bacon
1 cup melted butter
1 cup chicken broth
1 cup claret, burgundy or
sherry (optional)

Clean the goose, and then wash with salt water, rinse and pat dry inside and out. Stuff the cavity with your favorite stuffing, and sew it up. Rub the surface of the bird with salad oil. Mix the flour, salt, pepper, tarragon and thyme and dredge the bird. Sprinkle any remaining dredging mixture over the breast. Lay the thick slices of salt port or the bacon strips on the breast and tie in place with string. Place the goose in an uncovered roaster and roast in a 325° oven until tender, allowing 30 minutes per pound roasting time. Melt the butter in a small pot, add the chicken broth and wine or sherry if desired, and use it to baste the goose every 10 or 15 minutes during the cooking period. Remove the salt pork or bacon for the last 15 minutes of cooking time to allow the breast to brown.

Foothills Art Center

Continued

Foothills Art Center features changing exhibitions of painting, sculpture, and fine crafts by local, regional, and national artists. Classes are offered for children and adults. The Art Center is open Monday through Saturday from 10:00am - 5:00pm and on Sunday from 1:00pm to 5:00pm. Please be sure to visit our gift shop.

December 1858
Christmas Dinner in the Kansas Territory

Before Colorado was a state, it was in the Kansas territory. This was the first Christmas dinner served after the gold strike

Soup:

Oyster soup

Ox tail soup

Fish:

Salmon trout with oyster sauce

Boiled Meat:

Corned beef	Ham
Buffalo tongue	Pork
Mutton	Beef tongue
Elk tongue	

Roast:

Venison a la Mode	Pork
Smothered buffalo	Grizzly Bear a la Mode
Antelope	Elk
Beef	Mountain sheep
Mutton	Mountain pig

Game:

Mountain pheasants	Mountain rabbits
Turkeys	Ducks
Sage Hen	Prairie chickens
Black Mountain Squirrel	Prairie dog
Snipe	White Swans
Quail	Sand hill cranes

Extras:

Baked potatoes	Boiled potatoes
Rice	Baked beans
Boiled beans	Fried Beets
Fried squashes	Stewed pumpkins

Dessert:

Mince pie	Currant pie
Apple pie	Rice pie
Peach pie	Mountain-cranberry pie
Tapioca pudding	Bread pudding
Rice pudding	

Fruits:

Brazil nuts	Almonds
Hazel nuts	Filberts
Pecans	Wild currants
Raisins	Prickly pear
Dried mountain plums	

Wine List:

Hockheimer	Champagne
Madeira	Golden sherry
Cherry Bounce	Hock
Monogahela whiskey	Jamaica rum
Bourbon whiskey	Taos Lightning

Astor House Museum

822 12th Street Golden, CO 80401

303.278.3557

www.astorhousemuseum.org

Seth Lake built the Astor House in 1867 to attract the business of the territorial legislature when Golden City was Colorado's Territorial Capital. The building's stone walls symbolized permanence on the frontier, with Golden City serving as a key mining supply hub on the road to Blackhawk and Central City. When the capital moved to Denver in 1868, the Astor House became a boarding house, relying on more traditional patrons such as laborers, miners, travelers, and merchants.

Grouse with Orange Slices

4 grouse	chopped parsley
salt and pepper	¼ cup butter, melted
4 orange slices, ¼ inch thick, peeled and sliced	grated peel 1 orange
	2 tbsp. orange juice
4 slices bacon	1 tsp. lemon juice

Clean grouse. Sprinkle grouse inside and out with salt and pepper. Cover breast of each with an orange slice and a bacon slice, fasten with string. Place grouse, breasts up, in a baking dish. Roast in preheated 350º oven 40 - 50 minutes, or until tender. Combine butter, orange peel, orange juice and lemon juice and baste frequently. Remove string. Sprinkle with parsley. Serve with roasted orange and bacon slices. Serves 4.

Prairie Chicken Shortcake

Since prairie chicken is a protected species, we don't advocate using it for this dish; chicken works just as well.

3 cups cooked prairie chicken, cut up
2 tbsp. butter
2 tbsp. flour
1 cup milk
Large pinch dried herbs (options: basil, oregano, thyme)
Salt and pepper to taste

Melt butter in frying pan, add flour and brown. Add milk slowly and stir to keep from lumping. When thickened, add herbs, salt and pepper, and chicken. Sauté until warmed through. Serve over cornbread.

Pheasant Pie

2 pheasants
1 bay leaf
1 stalk celery
6 peppercorns
1 tbsp. salt
½ cup butter
½ cup flour
1 cup light cream
1/8 tsp. pepper

¼ tsp. salt
1 can pearl onions, drained
1 small can sliced mush
    rooms, drained
1 package frozen peas
2 canned pimientos, sliced
1 10-inch round of pastry

Continued
Today, visitors experience frontier Colorado life through the history of the Astor House, historic interiors, changing exhibitions, and hands-on activities. Listed on the National Register of Historic Places, the Astor House Museum is open for tours Tuesday through Saturday, 10:00am - 4:30pm. It hosts a popular series of Tea Time at the Astor House Museum education programs, and features a Victorian gift shop. Call for special summer hours and programs.

Clean and skin pheasants, wash thoroughly. Place pheasant in a large kettle and cover with water. Add bay leaf, celery, peppercorns and 1 tablespoon salt. Bring to boil. Cover, reduce heat and cook over low heat approximately 2 ½ hours, or until pheasant is tender. Remove meat from bones in fairly large pieces and set aside. Strain broth. Melt butter in a saucepan, add the flour and stir until blended. Gradually add 2 cups of the broth, stirring constantly. Add light cream, pepper and salt. Cook, stirring until thickened. Arrange pheasant pieces, onions, mushrooms, peas and pimientos in a 2-quart casserole. Add sauce, leaving at least 1-inch space on top. Prepare pastry. Cut pastry circle ½ inch larger than casserole and place over pheasant mixture, turning edge of pastry under and pressing to casserole with fork or spoon. Make a cut in the pastry to allow steam to escape. Bake in preheated 425° oven 15 minutes, or until crust is golden brown. Serves 6.

Roast Pheasant

2 pheasants
2 whole carrots, cleaned
2 whole onions, cleaned
2 stalks celery
2 tbsp. butter
1 tsp. salt
¼ tsp. pepper

Pluck and draw pheasants. Wash thoroughly inside and out, pat dry. Place a carrot, onion and a stalk of celery in each cavity. Spread butter over surface of birds and sprinkle with salt and pepper. Place in a covered roaster and bake in a 350° oven for 1 ½ hours, or until birds are tender. If birds seem very dry, add 1 cup boiling water to roaster. Remove vegetables from cavity and discard before serving. Serves 4.

Beaver Tail

This is a pioneer recipe gathered from an early resident of Colorado. It is just for fun!

Scald well; with a knife scrape off the black scales. Singe the hairs. Cook in heavy black kettle till tender, pouring off the water several times. Remove meat from tailbone. Meat is white and gelatinous. It may be used in a number of ways:

1. Serve whole on platter with lemon and butter sauce.
2. Cut into cubes and add to navy bean soup. Salt and pepper generously.
3. Pack cooked beaver tail in a crock, cover with hot pickling brine and let stand several hours. Pickling beaver tail is especially good to disguise the strong flavor if beaver have been eating too many willows.

Roast Beaver

Without a doubt, this is one of the tastiest ways to serve beaver!

1 beaver, skinned and cleaned
½ cup vinegar
1 tbsp. salt
2 tsp. salt
2 tsp. soda

1 medium onion, sliced
4 strips bacon or salt port
½ tsp. salt
¼ tsp. pepper

Wash beaver thoroughly with salt, water, then let soak overnight in enough cold water to cover. Add ½ cup vinegar and 1 tablespoon salt to the water. The next day, remove the beaver from the brine, wash and cover with a solution of 2 teaspoons soda to 2 quarts water. Bring to a boil, reduce heat and simmer 10 minutes. Drain, then place beaver in roasting pan. Cover with sliced onions and strips of bacon and season with salt and pepper. Place lid on roaster and bake in 375° oven until tender. Serve with a tart jelly. Serves 4.

Creole Rabbit

3 pounds rabbit (cut in serving pieces)
¼ cup milk
flour, salt and pepper
3 tbsp. cooking fat or oil

Creole Sauce:
2 medium onions, sliced
1 clove garlic, chopped fine
1 tablespoon chopped parsley
3 tablespoons butter, margarine or oil
3½ cups tomato juice
¼ tsp. Worcestershire sauce
salt and pepper to taste

Dip rabbit in milk and roll it in mixture of flour, salt and pepper. Heat fat or oil and brown rabbit on all sides lightly. To prepare sauce, cook onions, garlic and parsley in fat or oil until onion is golden brown. Add tomato juice and Worcestershire sauce and cook gently for 15 minutes. Season with salt and pepper to taste. Pour sauce over rabbit, cover pan. Bake in 325° oven 1 ½ hours, or until meat is tender. Uncover and bake 30 minutes longer to brown top. Serves 6.

Jugged Hare

1 hare
2 ounces cognac
2 tbsp. olive oil
½ tsp. salt
¼ tsp. pepper
1 medium onion, thinly sliced
1 pound lean side pork
2 tbsp. butter

1 clove garlic, minced
2 medium-sized onion, quartered
1 tbsp. flour
3 ounces red wine
1 bay leaf
1 tbsp. chopped parsley
1 tsp. thyme

Cut hare into serving pieces, wash and pat dry. Place the pieces of hare in a large bowl or earthenware pot. Mix the cognac, olive oil, salt, pepper, and sliced onion and pour over the meat. Let stand in the marinade for a few hours. Cut the side pork into small pieces and boil for a few minutes. Drain, then dredge with flour. Melt 2 tablespoons butter in heavy fry pan and sauté the pieces of pork and minced garlic until golden brown. Set aside. Dredge the quartered onion with flour and sauté until golden brown, add to the pork. Drain the pieces of hare, and sear them in hot fry pan. Pour 3 ounces of red wine over the meat and enough water to cover. Add the bay leaf, parsley and thyme and simmer until meat is tender. Place the cooked pork and onions in a serving dish and lay the pieces of hare on top. Pour the sauce over all and serve hot. Serves 4.

Squirrel Fricassee

1 squirrel
½ tsp. salt
1/8 tsp. pepper
½ cup flour

4 slices bacon, cut up
1 tbsp. diced onion
1 ½ tsp. lemon juice
1/3 cup broth

Skin and clean squirrel, being sure to remove scent glands from forelegs. Wash thoroughly and cut squirrel into serving pieces. Rub pieces with salt and pepper, then dredge with flour. Cut up bacon and cook over low heat till crisp. Add the squirrel and pan fry with the bacon for 20 minutes, until nicely browned. Add diced onion, lemon juice and broth. Cover tightly and simmer for 2 hours.

Jerky

2 lbs. lean beef, elk, bison, or venison*
1/3 cup Worcestershire sauce
1/3 cup soy sauce
1 tsp. onion powder
1 tsp. Accent seasoning (optional)
½ tsp. freshly ground black pepper
½ tsp. garlic powder
1 tsp. Liquid Smoke
dash Tabasco (optional)

Slice the meat into long, thin strips. Trim off fat. Mix remaining ingredients in a large bowl or plastic zipper close bag. Marinate the meat in the sauce in the bowl or plastic bag overnight.

Place the strips on an old barbeque grill out in the sun all day. Turn the pieces midday. To deter flies, cover the meat with an old piece of window screen. As an alternative, place the meat on a rack in the oven at 250° for several hours. Store in refrigerator.

* Rump roasts, flank steak or round steak cuts are good choices.

Goosefoot with Mushrooms

Chenopodium, lambs-quarters, wild spinach, pigweed, or goosefoot, no matter what you call it, this plant is everywhere. If collecting it from a yard or public area, be certain to wash thoroughly before cooking.

4 tbsp. butter
½ cup onion, thinly sliced
½ cup fresh mushroom, sliced
2 cups goosefoot leaves and stems, chopped
¼ cup water

2 tbsp. flour
1 cup milk
salt and pepper to taste
½ cup sour cream (optional)

Melt butter in a large skillet, sauté onions and mushrooms until tender. Add goosefoot and water. Cover and cook over medium heat until leaves are tender and bright green, about 5 minutes. Remove lid. Shift ingredients to one side of pan tilt skillet so that butter runs to one side. Blend flour with butter, cook and stir until mixture bubbles. Add milk and stir until thickened. Season to taste. Stir in sour cream. Serve over rice or potatoes.

Serviceberry Puffs

Once a staple food for the Native Americans, the serviceberry can still be found growing wild in the mountains of Colorado. Harvest the berries in mid-summer.

½ cup butter
1 cup water
4 eggs
½ cup flour
½ cup whole wheat flour
½ cup fresh service berries
2 tbsp. grated orange peel
Frosting:
½ stick butter, softened
1½ cups powdered sugar
2 tbsp. boiling water
1 tsp. vanilla
2 tbsp. grated orange peel

Preheat oven to 425°. Grease a cookie sheet. Stir together flours and set aside. Melt butter in the water in a saucepan over medium-high heat. When the water boils, turn to low and add the flour. Stir quickly to incorporate until mixture holds together, about 1 minute. Remove from heat and cool for 1 minute. Add the eggs one at a time, beating well. Stir in berries and orange peel. Drop batter by tablespoonfuls onto cookie sheet. Bake for 15 minutes, then reduce heat to 325° and bake for another 25 minutes or until golden brown. Remove from oven, cool slightly on wire rack. Frost while still warm.

Frosting: In a mixing bowl, beat butter, sugar and water until creamy. Add vanilla and orange rind.

Pickled Cactus Relish

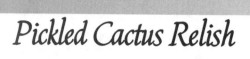

Prickly pear is a terrific plant. Both the pads and the bright red fruit are edible. It is available in some supermarkets now, but freshly collected is the best. Use thick gloves, tongs, and a sharp knife when collecting. Sear the spines off over an open flame. Pads are generally boiled or roasted until soft.

1 tbsp. pickling spices
1½ cups cooked, chopped cactus pad
¾ cup chopped onion
¾ cup cider vinegar
¼ cup water
½ cup sugar
½ tsp. salt
1 tbsp. mustard seed

Tie the pickling spices into a small square of cheesecloth. Place all ingredients and spice bag into a large pot over medium-low heat. Cook for 10 minutes, then remove from heat, cover, and allow to cool about 4 hours. Remove spice bag and discard. Stir well and transfer to storage containers. Store in refrigerator up to 2 months.

Home Remedies

Born in 1846, William F. Cody was the Wild West! He herded cattle, worked on a wagon train, mined for gold, rode for the Pony Express, and scouted for the Army. His skill as a buffalo hunter gained him the nickname "Buffalo Bill." Cody used his fame as a symbol of the Western spirit to establish "Buffalo Bill's Wild West," one of the greatest show business legacies in the world. Cody's exhibition traveled all over the world, teaching people about life in the American West. When Cody died in 1917 over 20,000 well-wishers attended his funeral atop Golden's Lookout Mountain. Cody had chosen this location because of its spectacular view. From the grave site, visitors can enjoy the two landscapes that played such a significant part in his life: the Rocky Mountains and the Great Plains. The site remains one of the most scenic vistas in the Golden area.

(Photo: William F. "Buffalo Bill" Cody, c.1880; courtesy of the Golden Pioneer Museum)

Mother's Cough Syrup

Half an ounce of Horehound, one ounce of licorice root, and half a tea-cup of Flax-seed. Boil them in three pints of water down to a pint, and sweeten well with honey or loaf sugar, add sufficient spirit to keep it if you please.

Cold Cure

One ounce each of licorice root, thoroughwort, flax seed, and slippery elm bark. Cut the elm bark and licorice root up fine, mix with the water; steep slowly for ten hours. Strain, and add to the sirup one pound of loaf sugar and one pint of molasses; boil for a few minutes and bottle. Take a tablespoonful four times a day.

Indigestion

1 pint boiled water
2 tsp baking soda
2 tsp aromatic spirit ammonia
2 tsp peppermint

Mix well. Take 3 tsp for an upset stomach.

Cleaning Fluid for Woolen Goods and Marks on Furniture

4 ounces ammonia
2 ounces alcohol
2 ounces ether
4 ounces castile soap
2 ounces glycerin

Cut soap fine, dissolve in one quart water over the fire. Add four quarts water. When nearly cold add other ingredients. This will make eight quart. Put into a bottle and cork. To wash a dress: to a pail of lukewarm water, put a cup of the fluid, shake well, and rinse in plenty of water.

All-Purpose Cleaner

¼ cup baking soda
½ cup vinegar
1 cup ammonia

Add above ingredients to one gallon of water. It will clean most anything.

White Wash

Mix 5 parts of lime to 1 part of cement and keep well mixed up as you use it – water proof cement is best if you can get it, if not regular will make a good job.

Herbal Dyes

Herbal dyes work best with natural fibers such as unbleached cotton and wool. Gather the plants just before they come into flower. Chop plants roughly and place in a muslin bag. Steep in warm water overnight, and then boil until dye reaches the desired color strength. Wash fabric; soak it in a bath of alum or copper to fix color. Place fabric in dye until desire color is reached.

Blackberry – the young shoots prepared with alum produce creamy beige.
Comfrey – the leaves prepared with alum produce yellow.
Chamomile – The flowers prepared with alum and a pinch of cream of tartar produce a bright yellow; with a copper bath and a pinch of acetic acid produce olive green.
Elder – the berries prepared with alum and a pinch of salt produce purple.
Juniper – the fresh berries prepared in alum produce deep yellow; prepared in a copper bath with cream of tartar produce olive-brown.
Madder – prepared with alum and a pinch of cream of tartar produces bright red.
Sorrel – the root prepared with alum produce rose pink; the leaves produce buff.
Tansy – the flowering tops produce mustard yellow.

Colorado Railroad Museum

17155 W. 44th Avenue
Golden, CO 80401
800.365.6263
www.crrm.org

Nestled between the magnificent heights of North and South Table Mountains in east Golden is the Colorado Railroad Museum. The Museum was established in 1959 to preserve for future generations a tangible record of Colorado's flamboyant railroad era, particularly the state's pioneering narrow gauge mountain railroads.

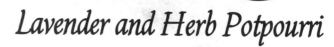

Lavender and Herb Potpourri

1 cup lavender flowers, dried
1 cup sweet herb leaves, such as Bay, lemon verbena, hyssop, lemon balm, or pineapple sage
½ cup chamomile flowers, dried
½ cup violet or pansy flowers, dried
1 tsp orange peel, dried and finely shredded
1 oz. orris root powder
½ tsp. grated nutmeg
½ tsp. cloves, finely crushed
3 drops lavender oil
1 drop rose-geranium oil

Gently mix together all the ingredients, do not crush the flower heads. Cover tightly and leave in a warm place 2 to 3 weeks until the scents have blended. Transfer to a shallow bowl or lined basket.

Homemade Modeling Clay

Make one recipe for each color desired. Dough may be divided for smaller batches or multiple colors.

Combine in order:
2½ cups unbleached all purpose flour
½ cup salt
3 tbsp. corn or vegetable oil
1 tbsp. alum
1¾ - 2 cups boiling water

Stir together. Add food coloring to create desired hue. Mix thoroughly, kneading if necessary. Store in an airtight container.

Bath Bags

These wonderful little bags can be used as a skin exfoliant by rubbing them directly on the skin, or as a bath additive by holding beneath the tap while filling the tub. Mix together the basic ingredients, then add one of the following "flavors": astringent, fresh, or soothing.

Basic Ingredients:
8oz grated soap containing essential oils (such as tea tree, lavender, etc.)

2 oz. corn meal

2 oz. oatmeal

1 oz. ground almonds (almond meal)

Astringent:
½ tsp. dried lavender flowers

½ tsp. fresh rosemary leaves

1 drop chamomile essential oil

Fresh:
¼ tsp. dried and powdered orange peel

¼ tsp. dried and powdered lemon peel

1 tsp. dried rose petals

1 drop geranium essential oil

Soothing:
½ tsp. dried calendula (marigold) petals

½ tsp. grated cocoa butter

4 drops wheat germ oil

Mix ingredients together and place 1 tbsp. inside a 6-inch square of muslin, draw up the corners and tie with a length of colorfast ribbon or raffia.

Continued

The 15-acre site boasts a 5-stall roundhouse complete with inspection pit and machine shop where restoration on its many engines and train cars is conducted. Over 70 railroad exhibits guide the visitor through the fascinating history of railroading in Colorado. Come explore the Denver & Grande Western #60 Post Office Car from 1899, or maybe the Denver & Rio Grande 346 2-8-0 Baldwin narrow gauge steam engine is more to your liking. Periodic steam-ups of the vintage engines are always a good time. Guaranteed to spark a life-long love of trains in any visitor. The Museum also has a research library and gift shop. Hours are daily 9:00am - 5:00pm, summer hours until 6:00pm.

Buffalo Bill Memorial Museum & Grave

987½ Lookout Mountain
Parkway
Golden, CO 80401
303.526.0744
www.buffalobill.org

Born in 1846, William F. "Buffalo Bill" Cody experienced the Old West to its fullest. When he died in 1917, the world mourned his passing. He was buried atop Lookout Mountain, outside Golden, Colorado. The Buffalo Bill Memorial Museum was built adjacent to the grave in 1921. Johnny Baker, a marksman with the Wild West shows and Buffalo Bill's foster son, started the museum to house mementoes from Cody's life and the Wild West. Because of his relationship to Buffalo Bill, he was able to collect many items from Cody's life as well as to compile the largest collection of Wild West show posters in existence.

Bath Fizzies

These are just like the expensive brand name fizzies, but you can tailor them to your favorite scent and color.

2 oz. cocoa butter
2 oz. baking soda
1 oz. citric acid
3 tbsp. cornmeal
6 drops food coloring
6 drops essential oil of your choice (such as ylang-ylang or rose)

Grease some small molds or an ice cube tray with non-stick cooking spray. Melt the cocoa butter in a double boiler over low heat. Remove from heat; add baking soda, citric acid, and cornmeal. Stir. Add the food coloring and essential oil. Stir well. Spoon into molds and place in freezer several hours to set. When hard, remove from molds. Drop one into a warm bath and relax!

Bath Oil

This is a lovely layered oil that will soothe your skin and make it silky soft.

4 drops liquid food coloring
2 oz. distilled water
4 drops essential oil of your choice (lavender, peppermint, or
    eucalyptus are good)
2 oz. almond oil

Add the food coloring to the water. Pour the essential oil into the almond oil. Gently pour the colored water into a clear glass bottle, and then top with the perfumed almond oil. Shake before pouring into bath water.

Hand Lotion

3 oz. glycerin
7 ounces water
5 to 10 drops carbolic acid
several drops of perfume

Mix all ingredients well.
Store in a tightly closed bottle.

Buffalo Bill Memorial Museum & Grave

Continued
Today the original museum building, designated a National Historic Landmark, is part of the Denver Mountain Parks system. The original building has since been converted into a gift shop, Pahaska Tepee, and a new building was created to house hundreds of new objects. Museum hours are Daily May - October, 9:00am - 5:00pm and Tuesday - Sunday November - April 9:00am - 4:00pm.

Substitutions and Equivalencies

1 cup whole milk = ½ cup evaporated milk and ½ cup water, or
    4 tbsp powdered milk and 1 cup water

1 cup sour milk = 1 cup sweet milk and 1 tbsp lemon juice or vinegar

1 cup butter = 7/8 cup cottonseed, corn or nut oil

1 tbsp cornstarch (for thickening) = 2 tbsp flour

1 square unsweetened chocolate = 3 tbsp. cocoa plus ½ tbsp shortening

1 cup sifted cake flour = 1 cup minus 2 tbsp sifted all purpose flour

1 whole egg = 2 egg yolks plus 1 tbsp water

1 cup molasses = 1 cup honey

1 cup granulated sugar = 1 1/3 cup brown sugar, or 1 ½ cup powdered sugar

1 tsp baking powder = ¼ tsp baking soda plus ½ tsp cream of tartar

15 graham crackers = 1 cup crumbs

23 saltines = 1 cup crumbs

1 orange rind = 2 tbsp grated

1 lemon rind = 1 tbsp grated